MODERN
LURE FISHING

MODERN LURE FISHING

Barrie Rickards

THE CROWOOD PRESS

First published in 2008 by
The Crowood Press Ltd
Ramsbury, Marlborough
Wiltshire SN8 2HR

www.crowood.com

© Barrie Rickards 2008

British Library Cataloguing-in-Publication Data
A catalogue record for this book is available from the British
Library.

ISBN 978 1 84797 065 7

Unless otherwise stated, photographs are from Barrie Rickards'
collection.

Frontispiece: Author with a lure-caught, lean summer
Fenland pike.

Typeset in Plantin by Bookcraft, Stroud, Goucestershire

Printed and bound in Malaysia by Times Offset (M) Sdn Bhd

Contents

Foreword – John Wilson   6
Acknowledgements   8
Introduction   9

1   The Lures   13
2   Tackle and Techniques   32
3   Pike on Lures   39
4   Boats and Big Waters – James Holgate   48
5   Jerkbait Fishing   61
6   Rubber Jigs and Lures   65
7   Advanced Big-Water Trolling – Gordon Burton   68
8   Lightweight Lure Fishing   81
9   Chub, Perch and Other Coarse Fish Species   84
10   Zander   89
11   Game Fishing: Salmon – Dave Steuart   91
12   Game Fishing: Trout – Fred J. Taylor   105
13   Game Fishing: Sea Trout   116
14   Big Game Fishing – David Bird   120
15   Sea Fishing   132
16   Flies and Lures   137
17   The Travelling Lure Angler   141

Bibliography   148
Useful Addresses   150
Index   153

Foreword

Barrie Rickards and his team of guest writers, most of whom I'm proud to say have been valued friends of us both for many years, have put together the best and most authoritative volume concerning artificial lure fishing from both bank and boat that I have ever read. Make no mistake, what you are about to enjoy and will no doubt refer to again and again is a most comprehensive work indeed, that is not only inspirational throughout (I defy anyone, for instance, to read Gordon Burton's section on 'Advanced Big-Water Trolling' and not want immediately to get out in a boat on a wild, open loch). The book is exciting in its coverage of lure fishing but is also solidly instructional, as well as being thought-provoking.

Like Barrie, I have also been a life-long lure enthusiast, with bass of 12lb, cod of 34lb, coalfish of 17lb, pike of 25lb, zander of 11lb, Chinook salmon of 30lb, lake trout of 33lb, vundu of 60lb, amberjack of 65lb, Nile perch of 150lb and big-eyed tuna of 220lb, plus many, many more species, all coming to lures. So I have countless good reasons to think the way I do and over the past couple of decades parts of mine and Barrie's angling lives have followed similar paths in that we have both been privileged to spend much time on the wild, massive expanse of Egypt's mysterious River Nile in the form of Lake Nasser, which for 300 miles stretches from the high dam in Aswan, all the way south into the Sudan. Not, I'm pleased to say, without our share

of 100lb+ monsters from both boats and the shore. And as most of the fishing for tiger fish and Nile perch in the Nile itself and on Lake Nasser is with artificial lures, I am sure Barrie would agree that so much has been learnt from watching the reactions of these fish to lures worked through the clear water of the lake, both from the

Dusk on any water is a good time for lures and pike.

boats and from the shore, and from the swirling waters of mother Nile herself below magnificent Murchison Falls. It has been a truly wonderful education. Who would imagine, for instance, that a gentle tap on the rod tip when trolling a 10in plug would come from a 100lb+ Nile perch that merely saunters up to the lure being trolled at between three to four knots, and nuts it with its forehead, gill plate or shoulder, as if to say, 'OK! Try getting away and I'll nail you.' To the angler, therefore, any gentle tap could mature into a most worthwhile catch, simply by instantly dropping back the lure (one of many reasons why multipliers are so superior to fixed spool reels for working lures) and then cranking it fast forwards in 'getaway' fashion. How I wish I had a £10 note for every good fish that has come my way simply by doing this! Which comes, of course, as do so many little tricks, from visually interpreting a predator's reaction through clear water. Conversely, that gentle tap could be from 4lb tigerfish doing likewise, which for much of the time is the case. However, as you try to kid a wild animal that your concoction of tin, brass, wood, aluminium, plastic or rubber is a worthwhile meal, you cannot take that chance by ignoring any reaction,

be it a single tap or a persistent series of seemingly inconsequential knocks.

This reminds me of a situation some years back when I was in Denmark with my old mate and fellow angling writer Dave Lewis, making one of my *Go Fishing* programmes for Anglia TV about catching sea trout. Whilst trolling up to half a mile offshore at around two to three knots in eighteen to twenty feet of crystal clear water, our J11 and J13 Rapala jointed plugs (working about four to five feet beneath the surface) were constantly being 'banged', but gently, and with no sea trout to follow. I hinted to Dave that maybe they were cod. 'No,' says Dave, 'you don't catch cod trolling.' Well, to cut a long and frustrating afternoon's trolling short, we accounted for a dozen or more beautifully marked cod in the 3–6lb range (plus a single sea trout) simply by dropping our lures back following the first tap or knock. Enough said. (Though I would never have believed those cod would come so far off the bottom and actually give chase.) But enough of what I think. Relax and enjoy what top experts of the day have to say about modern lure fishing. It's quite considerable.

John Wilson

Acknowledgements

I'm grateful for a great deal of help with the writing of this book, in particular James Holgate, who wrote Chapter 4, 'Boats and Big Waters', but also Gordon Burton, who has written on subjects about which he knows a great deal more than I do and penned Chapter 7, 'Advanced Big-Water Trolling' for this book. Dave Steuart very kindly allowed me to use some of his past writing, which he has added to, so as to make it as up to date now as when he originally penned it. This forms Chapter 11, 'Game Fishing: Salmon'. Similarly, the grand old man of angling, Fred J. Taylor, let me reuse his piece on spinning for trout, which is incomparable: I have introduced it with a few words of my own as Chapter 12, 'Game Fishing: Trout'. And David Bird I dragged kicking and screaming out of his retirement paddock to tell us a bit about big game fishing, which anglers are increasingly turning to; indeed, are increasingly able to afford. The result is Chapter 14, 'Big Game Fishing'. All the above have helped with photographs and diagrams. I am also extremely grateful to Rebecca Lyne for turning our crude sketches into works of art. Others have helped with pictures too: Bill Winship, John Milford, Eric Weight, and Dave Lumb. And finally Wendy Green, as always, has coped bravely with thousands of words of my handwriting to produce something others could read.

Author with a big, lure-caught zander, September 2008.

Introduction

Thirty years ago no angler would have imagined the extent to which lure fishing has now taken off – coarse, sea, game and big game. True, there had been glimmerings of hope, such as the famous Wagstaffe and Reynolds era of a few short years, and before that there was Thurlow Craig and his classic 1951 work *Spinners' Delight*. But these phases came and went and did not *electrify* the sport. The UK remained way, way behind the USA in particular. Tackle dealers did their best by importing a range of lures, most notably Ken Latham of Potter Heigham in the Norfolk Broads, who was a lure fisherman himself. The Shakespeare company always ran a small stable of successful lures, such as the Big S, for example. However, many lure sources faded and only a few individual anglers had the enterprise to order for themselves direct from the USA. I did this myself. There was still a caucus of lure anglers around, writing occasional articles, even books, such as Clive Gammon, Mike Prorok, Fred J. Taylor, Gordon Burton, Ray Webb, and some sea anglers too. But I think the 1950 revolution caused by Dick Walker and friends tended to put bait fishing to the fore in all fishing, not just pike fishing. I began lure fishing myself in the mid-1950s and have continued without break until now; at times it felt a bit lonely. At times it *was* lonely.

If I were to pinpoint the moment when lure fishing took off, when a range of good lures became available for the first time in the history of UK angling, when anglers

The author stalking trout: small lure rod, small lures, small stream, small trout.

Small cousin of the barracuda, Australia's barracuda. This one fell to a Tasmanian Devil lure.

began to chuck lures all over the country, it would be when Graham Easton and John Milford formed the T.G. Lure Company, in the mid-1980s. They not only imported vast quantities of lures from the USA and elsewhere, but their personal fanaticism inspired others very quickly. They were aided from the start by various close friends including Chris Leibbrandt and Steve Gould, the latter's Mohican hairstyle doing wonders for lure fishing. Within a year of those anglers getting together, everybody seemed to be chucking lures. In the Fens, where in the past you might see three lure anglers in a winter, now you'd see dozens on a weekend. Very quickly, other tackle companies came in and were very successful, such as the Kilty Lure Company, New World Lures and Pearce Lures, which were all run by enthusiastic lure anglers. The infection spread like wildfire. Even the big tackle companies such as Shakespeare

increased their range of lures to help meet demand.

Some anglers think the boom is over, but it isn't. There may not be quite the same infectious atmosphere of the 1990s, but there is no real sign of a decline in availability of lures – if they are still selling well, then anglers are still lure fishing. Some anglers do avoid taking up lure fishing because, on the face of it, it seems complicated. This is the same psychology which stops some anglers taking up fly fishing. So they stay with bait fishing. However, one of the things which has dragged the reluctant bait fishers into lure fishing has been the success with pike on lures on trout reservoirs – this has focused a few minds somewhat.

However, there is another factor which has firmed up the lure fishing revolution and that was the formation of the Lure Anglers' Society (LAS) in 1992 by the anglers connected with the T.G. Lure Company and their friends. Now, the healthy feature of this club (*see* Appendix) is that it is not just about pike fishing; members fish for coarse, sea and game fish, so in the Society's journal you will find articles on spinning for pollack or bass next to articles on spinning for perch or trout. The Society also holds fish-ins, teach-ins, competitions, social events and an annual conference. It is this breadth which has, in my opinion, cemented lure angling in the UK. We'll never look back now.

I am often asked by anglers – and not just beginners – how they can take up lure fishing. Well, in the future I'll tell them to do two things: read this book and join the LAS (or one of the other relevant clubs, *see* Appendix). Reading this book will provide you with a basic grounding in all the major facets of the sport of lure angling, but it also points up the latest ideas, developments and problem areas. Joining the LAS will give you a social side, a circle of friends and helpers, as well as knowledge of the

The author stalking brown trout on a small stream on Kangaroo Island, Australia.

new developments and lures. Similarly, no serious lure angler should avoid subscribing to the monthly magazine *Pike and Predators*, because it is there that many of us try out our daft ideas on you. James Holgate (*see* Chapter 4) is its editor. And do go to the annual conventions of the LAS and the Pike Anglers' Club (PAC). Not only will you enjoy an excellent social occasion, but you can buy, often at very competitive prices, any lures you need, not to mention books like this one.

Lure fishing is easy, really, so nobody should be put off. It's also very successful, and by that I mean with big fish as well as small. Let's take the misconception that lure fishing only catches small pike. This view held sway right through the second half of the previous century and is still a view held by many today. It is incorrect. It is true that you'll catch plenty of small pike on lures and in that it allies with livebaiting and contrasts with deadbaiting, where the *average* size of fish is high. But you'll catch just as many big pike as you will by bait fishing. I know this because I once analysed my catches of 20lb+ pike (at that stage around 200) and although more of them

fell to baits than lures, I had to remember that when bait fishing I'd usually be using three rods (today I use one or two only). When lure fishing, I'd only use one rod (even when trolling). So the bait fishing results had to be divided by three to effect a fair comparison. When I did that I got a surprise: slightly more 20lb fish had come to lures.

What applies to pike applies to many other species too, so lure fishing does produce big fish, although for most lure fishermen that doesn't seem to matter a great deal. Certainly it does not to me. There are just two species where I do wonder if baits produce the larger fish namely perch and chub. These are particularly wised-up species and not many *really* big ones of either seem to fall to lures.

In this book, I have tried to give a flavour of the great range of the sport and also to cover the tackle and tactics needed to make a start. To some extent, I have viewed it from the position of a coarse angler taking up lure fishing and then moving on from pike, perch and zander to sea fishing, trout fishing, salmon fishing, and so on. All things are possible with only a little modification

Many species fall prey to lures, as did this small fish on the Amazon – to a Big S plug.

of gear or of thinking. I've done it this way because game and sea anglers seem able to take up freshwater lure fishing more readily than the other way round.

I begin with the lures themselves because they are, after all, rather fundamental to the art and science of lure fishing. They are what defines the sport and many anglers love lures for themselves – never mind the fishing. I move on then to the essential tackle and basic techniques, this being the only area where a slightly different mindset to other forms of fishing needs to be developed, one that underpins all lure fishing. From there it is but a short step for the newcomer to try a bit of pike lure fishing, hence Chapter 3. The angler will have plenty of potential pike fishing nearby and is certain quickly to get a nice fish or two, thus rapidly boosting his confidence.

After that, in Chapter 4, I introduce boat fishing through the highly experienced pen of James Holgate, possibly the country's leading exponent of boat fishing and modern boating techniques. Being happy in a boat, of course, makes a lot more fishing available – for example sea fishing, big game, Nile perch, salmon – which I cover later in the book. Then follows four chapters dealing with some very modern developments that have a wider application other than to just pike. After that, I briefly cover the various species the lure fisherman might commonly chase and then end with a subject which also, to a large degree, defines the lure angler, to whit the mobile aspect of it (Chapter 17). To quite a number of anglers lure fishing is the be all and end all of angling, because its scope is so vast. But to others, including me, it is a most pleasant addition to our armoury, and this book is written in that spirit.

Author spinning for cocky salmon on Victoria's coast, southeast Australia.

1 The Lures

The first thing which strikes a would-be lure angler is undoubtedly the enormous range of lures available: hundreds of styles in literally thousands of different sizes and colours. This was not the case half a century ago when I began lure fishing. At that time, each of the main branches of the sport – coarse, sea and game angling – had little more than half a dozen types for each available to the angler. Many were, and are, very famous names such as Colorado and kidney spoons, Norwich spoons, quill minnows, and so on. Today, however, we have this huge array of lures, a direct consequence of the lure fishing revolution referred to in the Introduction. Some think it is an acme, that we shall never see such a glut of lures again, that the bubble must burst and the manufacturers will suffer a downturn. There are no indications of this as yet. Lure fishing itself seems to go from strength to strength and is certainly a more diverse pastime today than ever in the past. Even if the peak did come, and pass, what better excuse than to buy up a good selection of lures now?

Where to start? A little later in this chapter I'll debate the principal types of lures and their main functions, but for the moment let's think in terms of an angler wanting to get stuck in and get on with it. Most anglers are impatient. If you go into a suitable tackle shop, one obviously well stocked with lures, or attend a tackle show similarly stocked, the thing to do is ask for help from the dealer and then buy a *variety* of plugs, spoons and spinners. Buy as many as you can afford, within reason. As a rough guide, if your bag of purchases seems rather heavy for a long walk down the bank then you've probably overdone it. Half a dozen of each might suffice, but a dozen of each would be better. You might have to spend £100, so prepare yourself for that. I make the point this way because there is nothing worse than starting out with just one or two plugs or spinners, spending a day at the water and either having a blank or losing your lures. Or, perhaps, finding that the ones you have don't really work well

Cantilever boxes used for lure storage, and perhaps for boat fishing, but excessively cumbersome on the banks.

A typical angling show replete with lures galore. Here Steve Gould of the legendary T.G. Lures holds the fort.

on your chosen waters. Of course, you'll have told the dealer your water types and if you have a range of lures, rather than a handful, you'll probably find something that does work well; one that casts into that bad wind, one that goes deep, or one that defeats the snags or cuts through the weed. And remember, the predatory fish you are hunting can be finicky, in our experience often preferring, on the day, a particular size, colour or type of lure.

You may be setting out on this venture on your own, but it's much better if you can team up with someone who has done a bit, or knows the waters. This can help a lot with initial choice of lures – a good

Traditional crankbaits, poppers, worms and spoons.

starting point. But that is all it is, because anglers get set in their ways and it really is best to think things out for yourself, experiment and ring the changes. I'm told that I change lures every few minutes. While I don't think that is actually correct, especially when I believe I've found the 'going' lure for the day, it is true that I'm ready to change quickly if I'm not happy, and then I'll keep changing until I get it right. You can see from this that the more lures you can comfortably carry, the better your day's angling is likely to be.

At the beginning of this chapter, I mentioned plugs, spinners and spoons without defining what they were. This was quite deliberate because, as a beginner, you could walk into a tackle shop and those are the terms the dealer would quickly understand and be able to help you with. However, after a few minutes you'll begin to notice that lures don't just come in three types: some things seem to be intermediate; some seem oddball, unique. Where does it all end? There's no need to despair. All lure types grade into other lure types. Whilst most lures fall into the main categories I describe below, there are always a few intermediate ones which seem neither plug nor spinner; neither spinner nor spoon. But that's all they are: intermediates which some designer has proved work. A few do not readily fit any category – for example, you've bought a few spinners, perhaps bar spoons like Veltic or Mepps or Shakespeares (*see* Figures) and you have the idea of a blade spinning around a shaft. Then you look at a spinnerbait, the lure often derisively called a coat hanger, and you realize it isn't really a spinner, it isn't a spoon (though it has a spoon blade as part of the assembly) and it certainly ain't a plug! It's a one-off really. Then some spinners have flies on them (fly spoons too), some jigs have plastic curly tails, some plugs have spinning blades, and so on. Not to worry; all will have become clear by the end of this book.

And, whilst we are on this subject of 'classification' what is a lure anyway? We look at this question again in Chapters 12,

Rapala Super Shad Raps display the ranges of colours available in today's lures. Red heads and gold may look unnatural, but on their day can outfish everything else.

Deep runners, with the shallow vanes: Salmo jerkbait, banana wobbler (green) and small and large metal Russelures, which are plugs, to the left.

13 and 16, but for the moment will simply note that the word lure is used in two quite different ways. One usage is that of the game or fly fisherman who describes his (usually) large flies as lures (polystrickles, babydolls, and so on). These are not really flies and do not often resemble natural flies or traditional fly patterns, but are concoctions of fur and feather, plus a few other things. Our usage, however, is rather different: we mean assemblages of wood, metal and plastic, plus softer additives, that are made to behave like fish. We are not imitating a fly hatch, but various kinds of fish (some quite imaginary!), or perhaps frogs and small mammals. So there is a difference between the lures of the fly fisherman and the lures in this book. Do not, therefore, go into a game fishing shop and ask for lures. That said, you will see in Chapter 13 on sea trout fishing, that there *are* lures which one would be hard-pressed to put in either category.

What, then, are the main types of lure available for anglers after predators?

Crankbaits

This is an unfortunate name, stemming from the USA in the 1990s, and seems to imply that you crank the reel handle and something happens to the lure. They used to be called floating divers or sinkers (now often called countdowns) and they are plugs. On the illustration of lures (*see* overleaf), look at the crankbaits and you will see a couple in action, one diving down from the surface (a) and one operating more deeply, having sunk there (b). Those that float (and dive when cranked) have a diving vane, or lip, at the front. If this lip points vertically downwards when the plug is at rest, then on the retrieve it will dive shallowly. If the lip is nearer to the horizontal when the plug is at rest, then on the retrieve it will dive more deeply. The bigger this near-horizontal diving vane is, the more deeply the plug will dive.

Sinking plugs can work in exactly the same way, and some, if you stop cranking, have neutral buoyancy and simply sit there

Some of the bigger lures: the Nilsmaster Invincibles in the centre are almost a foot long, as is the big Rapala lure on the left; the Ernie to the left of the Invincibles is a deep and vibrant worker.

in the water. You can vary greatly the dive rate of both floaters and divers and you can have different colours and sizes. Thus the combinations increase and it starts to become evident where all those thousands of lures come from. Are they all necessary? That will be examined from time to time as we progress, but the short answer is, yes, they are. Many crankbaits feature throughout this book, so I'm not going to name them all at this stage.

Floaters or Surface Baits

If you look at (a) to (f) on the illustration overleaf you will see several lures working away on the water surface – a Crazy Crawler heading to the lilies on the left and others to the right. Some surface lures work within the film at the surface (f) – standing upright when the retrieve is stopped and lurching forwards when the retrieve is started. Many surface lures have little blades which spin; others have arms which do the crawl and some have blades at the front which

enable them to 'pop' across the surface (called poppers). As with all lures, colours and sizes vary with the prey: for example, surface lures for pike might be 3–8in long, but for giant trevally on the Great Barrier Reef they might be 12in-long poppers. Many floaters give quite different actions and varied water disturbances. Some can be fished through weeds and snags, such as the floating frogs that can be worked in lily beds to great effect. Because the lure has to be taken off the surface by a predator it presupposes an active predator. You see the importance of this in pike angling when surface lures work well in summer, the pike's metabolism being high then, but less well in winter. So for pike you do better in winter with the subsurface categories.

By now, you'll be wondering whether there anything that cannot be done with lures. Well, at the moment I'm not aware of a lure that flies, but I've had pike several times take my lure after it had been lifted from the water and was hanging from the rod tip. A hovering lure might work, but I do not know of any. Finally in this section,

17

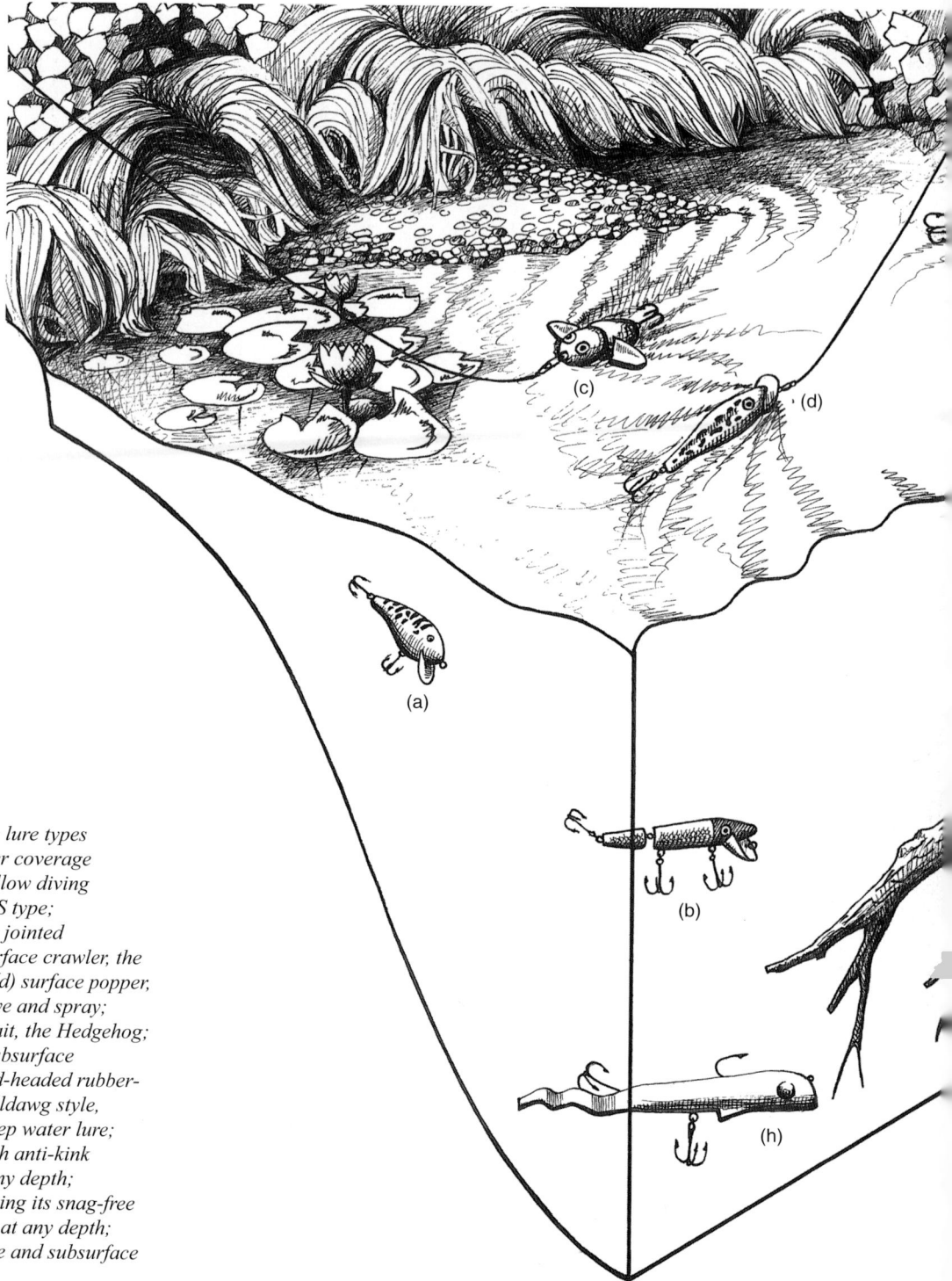

Some of the main lure types showing the water coverage possible: (a) shallow diving crankbait of Big S type; (b) deeper diving jointed crankbait; (c) surface crawler, the Crazy Crawler; (d) surface popper, creating bow wave and spray; (e) surface jerkbait, the Hedgehog; (f) surface and subsurface 'walker'; (g) lead-headed rubber-tailed jig; (h) Bulldawg style, rubber/plastic deep water lure; (i) bar spoon, with anti-kink weight, goes to any depth; (j) spinnerbait doing its snag-free job through logs, at any depth; (k) buzzer, surface and subsurface water disturber.

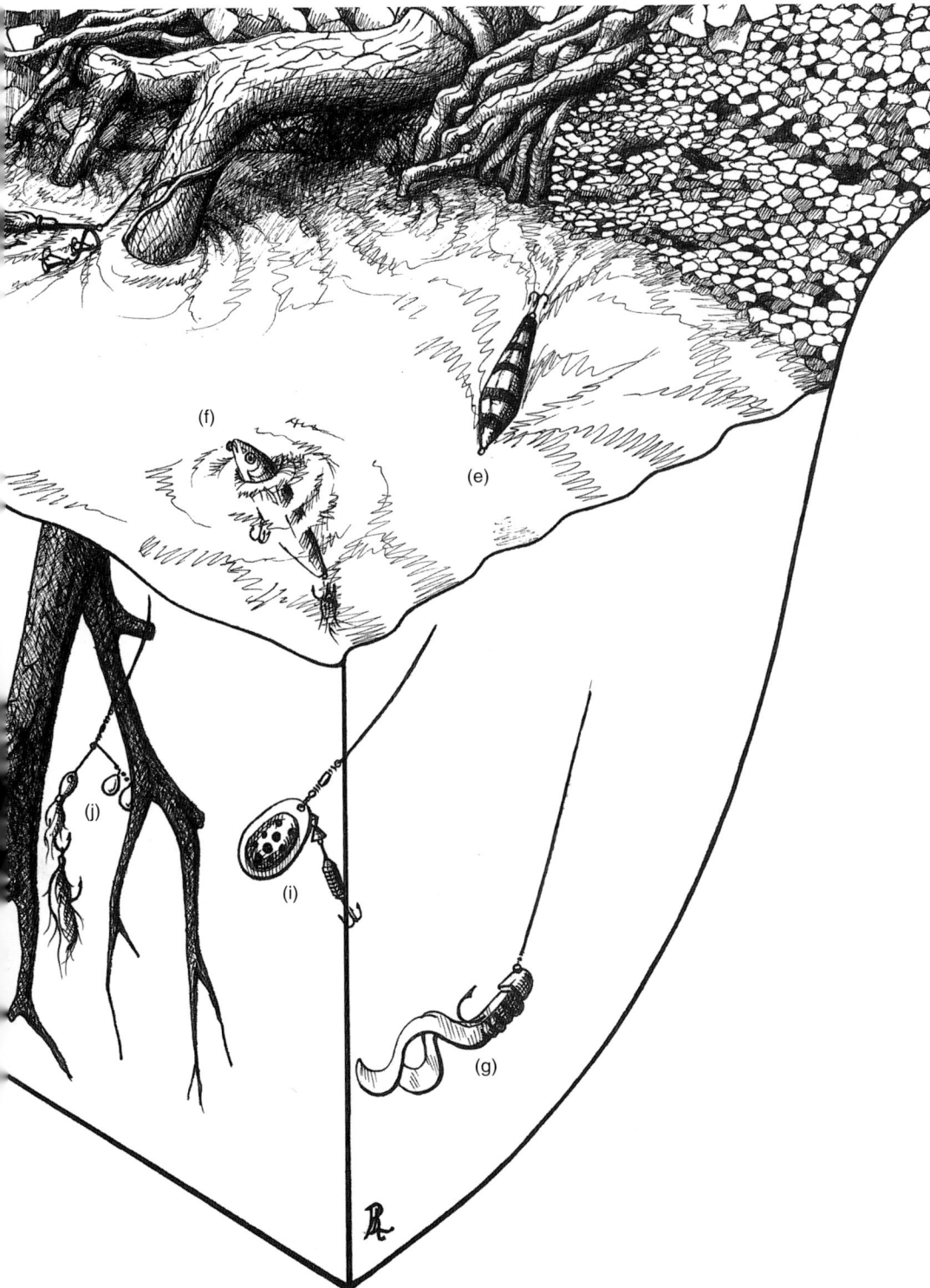

A selection of the huge range of rubber lures now available. This whole batch was simply lifted out of Barrie's travelling bucket.

if you lack a floater in your box, remember that a floating diver can be worked in the surface layers too. My best ever zander fell to this technique, after dark.

Jerkbaits

Jerkbait fishing is a specialist form of lure fishing. Jerkbaits are plugs, but, as their name implies, the rod is jerked to give them action. They lack the diving lip of crankbaits, so an erratic and jerky retrieve can be imparted by use of the rod tip. They can be both floaters (which may dive a little on the jerk) or sinkers. The first jerkbaits to reach this country from the USA, where they are used for muskies, were about 6in long, but since then they have grown much bigger. They do not have to be big though, and many anglers now use mini-jerkbaits and the appropriate tackle to fish them. The tackle necessary for comfortable jerkbait fishing is different from that used for other methods and will be covered in Chapter 5. The use of jerkbaits in the UK is relatively recent, beginning in the 1990s in a movement led by Malcolm Bannister and a few others. I recall Malcolm pressing on me a fistful of odd-looking plugs and telling me to get to it. They worked on the Fenland drains for pike from the word go, especially when the water had a bit of a blow on it. I have also used the Salmo range, successfully, for Nile perch and tigerfish, even though in general they do not seem to like jerkbaits much. I haven't put jerkbaits on the illustration, apart from the hedgehog, because there isn't room and I could not easily depict their action.

Squidgy Rubber Jobs and Jigs

I've used rubber lures since the 1970s and the possibilities are so huge that it's difficult to give them a single name. Some are just like countdown plugs, except that they are rubber (or some other synthetic soft material) and usually have a wiggly tail (h). Others are worms; some are jigs with a lead head and wiggly tail and rubber body

Detail of a rubber lure and jig selection.

(g). Some are crankbaits pure and simple but have soft 'rubber' bodies. We even used rubber eels and very long red worms in the 1970s. The one thing they have in common is a *soft* body. I'm convinced that the predator hangs onto them just a little bit longer because its jaws have clamped not on wood, metal or plastic, but on a soft body not unlike that of its normal prey. The other feature which most of them have is a rapid or wriggly action of the tail or tails. In Nile perch fishing this tends to result in good takes at a slow retrieve, whereas most lures have to be moved fast for that species. It must be the wriggly action which draws the strike, while the soft body makes them hold on longer.

Jigs are really a special category here. They have taken off in the UK in recent years, often as a result of the writings of Mick Brown, with pike and zander. They catch everything. The variations, in addition to size and colours, are achieved by using different weight heads and different sizes and shapes of wiggly bodies. Some anglers have recently concluded that if they

had to stick to just one lure it would be just this type. I can almost go along with that. They can be fished *almost* anywhere, anytime (*see* Chapters 2 and 3). Particular mention should be made, perhaps, of the big 'rubber' lures which have recently become very popular and effective, namely things like the Bulldawg. These cast well, hook well (sometimes *too* well) and can be fished at all depths. Their most attractive action is caused by their big wiggly tail; they have no diving lip and can be worked with a jerkbait-like motion if desired.

Perks I haven't yet discussed. These are metal weights with hooks on. They are primarily used at sea, but I've had pike on small ones. The sizes go up to over 1lb in weight when the angler is seriously cod fishing.

Spinners

To some extent spinners are the poor relations of the lure world, which is a pity. In piking circles they are not often used – again, a pity. It may simply be that they have

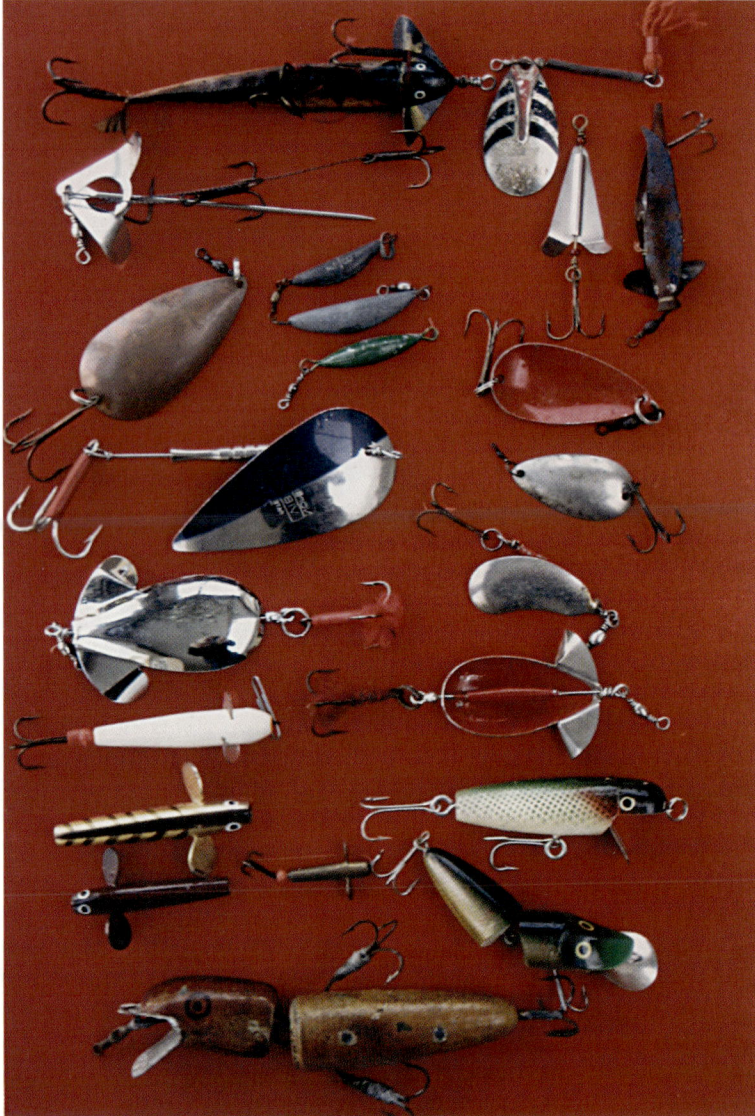

Classic lures which should not be neglected. Included here are wagtails, mackerel spinners, Norwich spoons, Vibros, Veltics, Kidney spoons, Colorados, minnows and plugs.

been around a long time and, along with spoons, were the mainstay of lure fishing in the first sixty years of the twentieth century. Anglers may be bored with them, but they still work well for a variety of species and most anglers have a few in their box or bag, albeit gathering dust and rust.

Most spinners have a blade rotating about an axis which is often weighted (i) and they'll have a treble hook or single hook beyond the weighted axis, depending upon the size of the lure. Spinners of this type are known as bar spoons and the overall size does not rise above a few inches because retrieve against the drag would be impossible; some big Vibro lures are hard work to pull in. Although smaller than many lures they do give off a

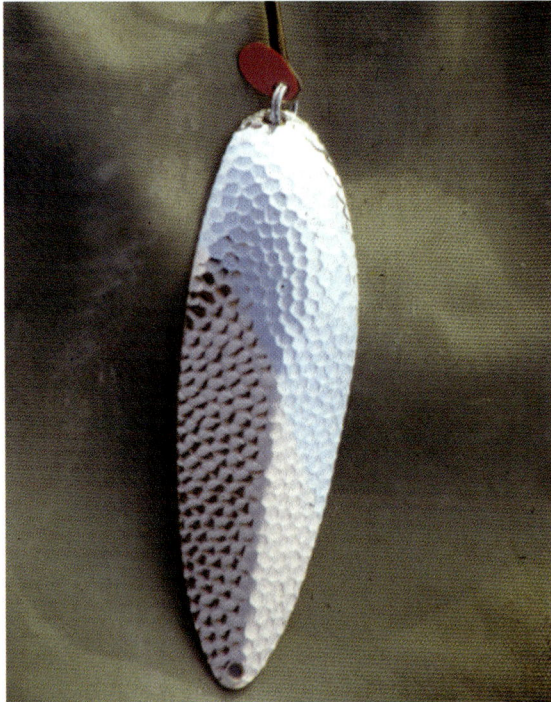

The Lucky Strike Lizard in copper and silver, the spoon on which Barrie took his best ever pike catch of more than 800lb in a day and a half.

disproportionate disturbance of the surrounding water, each spinner type creating its own specific vibration and fluid displacement pattern. Ken Whitehead and I, many years ago, investigated in a flume tank the vibration patterns of different lures and showed just how different they were (Rickards & Whitehead, 1987). Clearly, as well as colour and size, the vibration patterns will be important to the predator on particular days. Therefore, follow rule number one in lure fishing – ring the changes.

The disturbance caused by spinners when compared to most lures also introduces a problem we haven't yet met in the foregoing lure types. I refer to line twists. Most spinners twist up the line if an anti-kink lead or vane is not added, either just behind the lure itself or at the top of the trace when one is in use. In the case of tiny spinners this can simply be a swan shot clipped to the ring eye of the lure itself or to the link swivel, but often it needs to be large. I go for half-moon leads or Wye leads, preferring the latter. They *are* essential. They detract from the distance cast

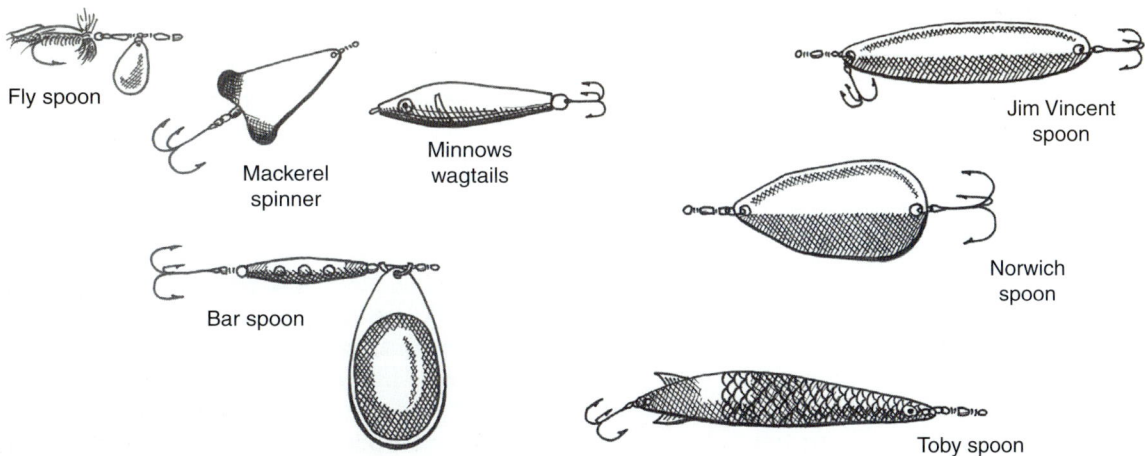

Fly spoon

Mackerel spinner

Minnows wagtails

Bar spoon

Jim Vincent spoon

Norwich spoon

Toby spoon

Some of the main types of spinners and spoons. Those towards the bottom of the diagram fish deeper.

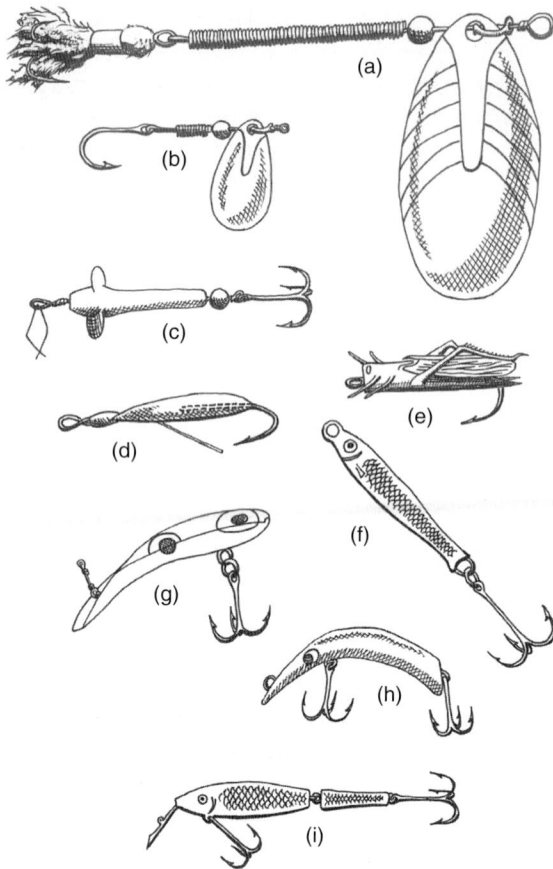

A range of 'old-fashioned' lures, still a power to be reckoned with: (a) Veltic- or Mepps-style bar spoon, one of the most versatile of lures; (b) basic fly spoon rig to which can be added feather, fur or rubber over the leaded shaft; (c) some of these minnows have reversible vanes which alternate the spin direction and prevent line twists; (d) 'weedless' spoon with bristle to protect the hook from snagging; (e) plastic grasshopper to fish under the rod top for chub; (f) small sea jig, can be straight or concavo-convex; (g) small deep-diving plug with erratic retrieve line; (h) famous banana plug comes in all sizes, tiny to trevally size, has a powerful action; (i) metal lure, half-perk half-crankbait, fishes deep.

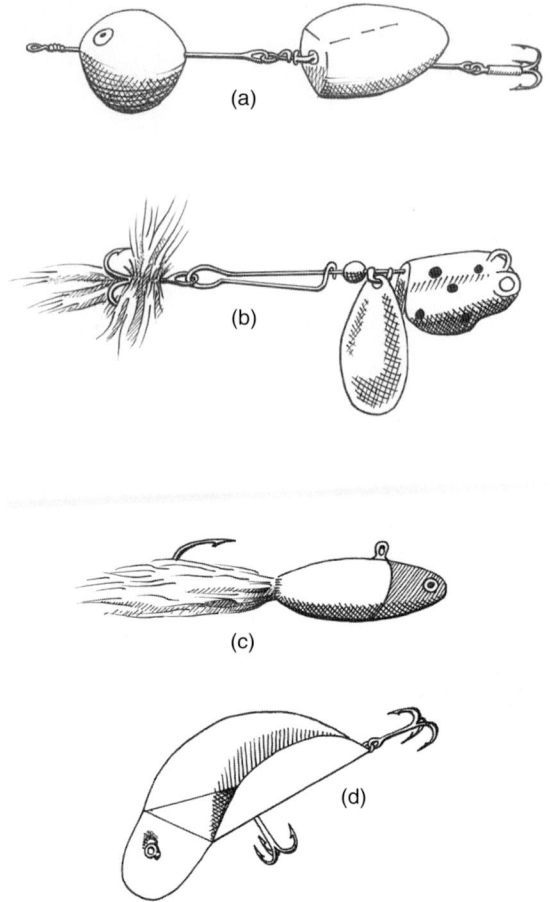

In-between lures: a) rubber head and trailing fly spoon, Ondex and Voblex do these; b) plastic, lead or rubber head coupled with both a bar spoon and a fly spoon; c) a feathered or woolled jig; d) a metal 'crankbait' or plug – really only fishable from a boat or a dam wall.

but that is a small price to pay. The alternative is a mess you may never be able to unravel. If you get it wrong and do end up with line twist, go out into a field some-where, pay off (walk off) all the line, *still with the spinner attached* and hooked into a sod (grass I mean), then unclip the spinner and walk the trailing line around the field for five minutes. That usually clears any problems. Then attach a brain.

Spinners are the unsung heroes of lure angling at present, but they can be highly effective. If you want to give them a try to gain confidence, try them on perch or wild trout (*see* Chapter 12). So far, I have only

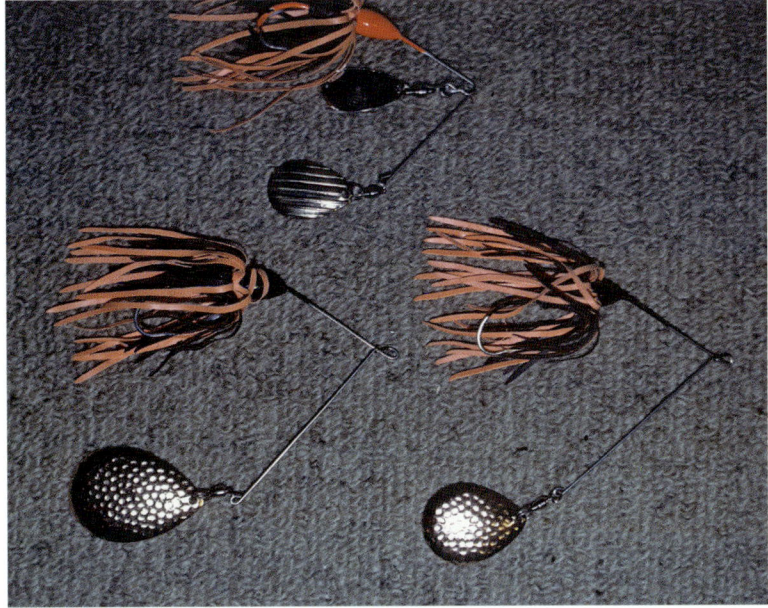

Barrie's Buzzers, introduced by Barrie and Bruce Vaughan at the start of, or perhaps the cause of, the spinnerbait revolution.

talked about the most widely used spinners, the bar spoons. But there are others such as minnows and mackerel 'spoons' (a misnomer you will see). In these the blade is replaced by making the body weight itself the imitation fish. They still cause line twist, or most of them do (some have reversible vanes to prevent this) so use an anti-kink device on them always. Their water disturbance is less than with bar spoons, but they come in the same size range and have bodies of plastic, wood, metal or rubber. The old-fashioned Wagtail is a minnow with a rubber body and tail fins.

The real Buzzer, below a heavy duty, two-bladed spinnerbait.

Spinnerbaits and Buzzers

For these lures, see (j) and (k) on the illustration on pages 18–19. Spinnerbaits are the coat hanger lures, so called because they comprise a V-shaped wire to the end of one arm of which is attached a skirt or tassel of material (with a lead inside) and to the other a spoon blade or blades. The hooks, usually single hooks of large size, are hidden in or project from the skirt. On retrieve they create the devil's own vibration. They cast like bullets and can be retrieved at *any* depth. They have, in their own way, helped to revolutionize lure fishing.

Their arrival into this country from the USA is interesting. As far as I can recall, the first ever mention of them was in an article by Fred J. Taylor many years go – nobody followed him up on it, he being ahead of his time as usual, and this failure to capitalize on his revelation was probably because bait fishing for pike was so successful at that time. Anglers in general could not see the point of lure fishing as it only caught little fish, didn't it? Then in the 1980s Bruce Vaughan obtained a boxful from the States and sent them to me as a joke, for 'field testing'. (I was a consultant for Ryobi in those days.) Anyway, I had a huge number of good pike on them in a couple of days, so, naturally, reported back favourably, much to Bruce's amazement. We decided to market one of them, which we called Barrie's Buzzer (a misnomer, as a result of incorrect labelling on the original packaging!) and sold 13,000 of them in a year. They caught on. Everyone laughed at them at first sight, but soon changed their tune when the fish started to come. I'd say spinnerbaits are generally better than most of the spinners of the previous section. But, like all lures, fish do 'go off' them.

One of the advantages of spinnerbaits is that as a rule they do not twist up the line. With single hooks they can be fished through snags like log stands and lily beds. In fact, in lily beds they can be deadly for pike. Fish do fall off the single hook more readily, but because of the overall more soft nature of the lure they'll often hit it again and again even if coming short. A stinger treble can be added to the single. I usually push a bit of valve rubber over the eye of the treble and then push the point of the single through the valve rubber. This ensures that the treble does not come off.

Once again, spinnerbaits are a versatile lure in that the lead size can be varied, the skirt colour changed, the spoon blades

A small, tight-wobbling, good diver, excellent on deeper drains and on rivers, especially under the banks. Note that despite a terminal spinnerbait-like blade this is a deep-diving crankbait.

Pikko lures, nice fishy-looking spoons which perform extremely well, either as single or in tandem when they take on a plug-like action.

can be one or several and of different sizes and colours. And, in place of the skirt, you could have a little rubber jig body – or whatever you fancy. Interestingly enough, some anglers swear that if they could only use one bait it would be the spinnerbait – rather like the rubber lure enthusiasts. But beware: my own experience is that fish on any one water go 'off' spinnerbaits in two seasons. One thing I am certain of, despite debate in some quarters, the predator attacks the spinnerbait skirt, not the spoon. Big fish engulf the lot so you may not be able to tell. The question is, why?

Buzzers are slightly different, and seem to have fallen out of favour recently. They are not unlike spinnerbaits (*see* (j) and (k) on pages 18–19 for the contrast) but the 'skirt' part tends to be in-line, and one or two little blades spin to one side of it. Each of these blades is rather like a mackerel spinner. They do not cast as well as spinnerbaits at the same sizes/weights and most of them fish shallow – you can buzz them superbly through the surface film, hence their name. I've had many fish on them, perch, pike and zander, and am surprised

to see them fall out of grace. Deep fishing them is not easy without sufficient lead. If the weight is too small they plane up to the top rather steeply, but this can be used as a ploy in itself if the rise is done slowly.

Renosky lures, with their fish facsimile on one side, have produced many zander for Barrie.

27

This is a team Barrie uses successfully on some very shallow, weeded gravel pits, the rooster tail spinner, top right, being fished beneath a float.

Spoons

These have been the main tool or the standby for predator fishers for so long now that knowledge about them is no doubt commonplace. I use them a great deal and

some of my biggest catches of fish have been on spoons, in the sea as well as freshwater. As a general rule, spoons do not tangle the line because they wobble rather than spin. However, any spoon can spin if the speed is increased past its working optimum, so it's a good idea to have a link swivel or swivel with ball bearings in it. Expensive but worth it.

There are some basic shapes of spoons, which make their design (and indeed description) easier than you might think when faced by a huge array. Firstly, there are the concavo-convex ones, like the Tobys. Then we have those which look like the spoon part of a dessert spoon – the so-called Norwich spoon. Those are concave on one side, convex on the other and tradition often paints them red on the concave part. Next we have an elongate version of the Norwich spoon, usually called the Vincent type (after Jim Vincent who used it on the Norfolk Broads). An example would be the Piker, but there are many others these days.

You can imagine how they vary. Increase the metal thickness and they cast to the horizon and sink like bricks. Decrease

The K12 Kwikfish in coachdog finish, top left, is, with the Barrie's Buzzer spinnerbait below it, one of the best lures in Fenland.

Big Kilty Lures spoons for trolling.

The famous 'Flying Condom', a kind of elongate bar spoon, alongside some Kitty Lures: big, heavy, distance spoons also good for trolling.

Big S with added eyes. Predators target eyes, so it may well help to increase the size of those provided by the lure makers.

the metal thickness and you have a spoon with a fluttering action (and hard to cast). Increase the size (length) of the spoon and you offer a big 'prey' to the predator. And the converse might be a tiny spoon for brook trout. And then there's the colour. Spoons have their protagonists, and rightly so. My old friend Tim Cole would use only spoons (often homemade) or spinnerbaits, nothing else, yet his catches were as good as anybody's, in itself food for thought. You can do *almost* anything with spoons that you can do with other lures, except perhaps fish in the surface film. What is needed there perhaps is a wooden spoon with a thin metal strip along one edge, but it hasn't happened to date I don't think …

The disturbance patterns of spoons are less and quite different from those of spinners (*see* Rickards & Whitehead, 1976, Bibliography). However, I did persuade one firm to produce, at least for testing, spoons with perforations all over them – I know this sounds odd, but the idea was to produce low-frequency vibrations. In this it succeeded, but whether they are better than other spoons it is too early to say.

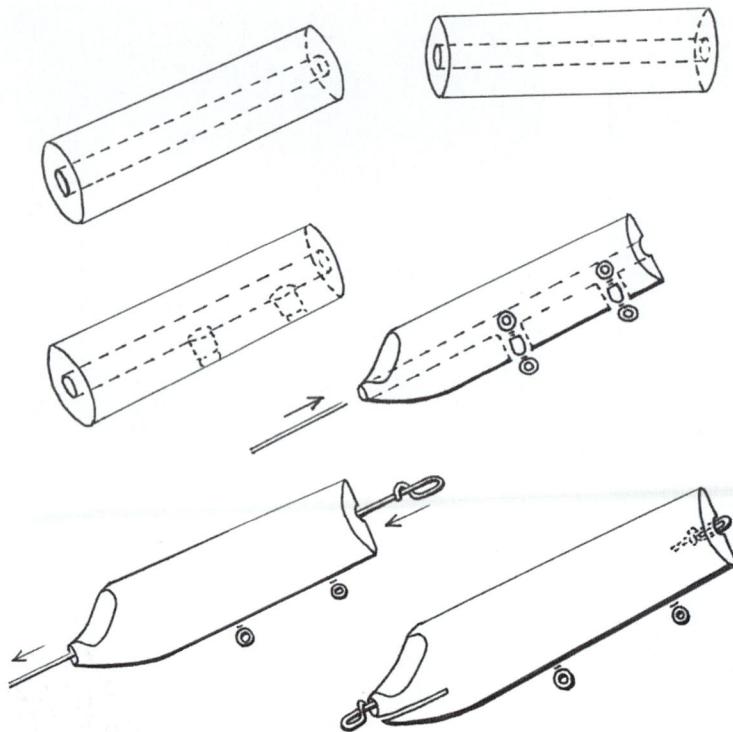

Basic stages in making a jointed, floating crankbait, the only difficult bit being the first long drill hole.

Experimental lures. The perforations in the spoon help it emit low-frequency vibrations.

Electric lures. These emit not only a tiny electric current, which predators home in on, but also a light which pulses every second or two.

And Finally

It cannot be emphasized too strongly that whilst most lures fall easily into the above categories, and your tackle shop man will know exactly what you need if you ask for them, quite a number are gradational or intermediate lure categories. These odd lures often have special features going for them so look out for them in the catalogues. Many of the lure types I have described are mentioned in the following text on many occasions and in pursuit of many different fish. Now you'll know what is being written about, especially if you scan the photographic illustrations which have been chosen to make our points.

Lure storage at home – always a nightmare. Here's one idea.

2 Tackle and Techniques

Tackle will, of course, be discussed in more detail in the chapters ahead, where it applies to a particular fish species or water. In this chapter, I cover the basic principles, in order to avoid some disappointments and pitfalls. For example, if you went into a shop and asked for a spinning rod, you might end up with anything. I will therefore start by talking about the rods a pike angler might need, rods which will deal with fish from a couple of pounds to over 30lb, and then go on to show how you need to change things to fish for other species and perhaps in environments which are 'rougher'.

For my piking I choose rods about 9ft long (for use with a fixed spool reel – *see* below). But the crucial thing is that they have a stiff or 'tippy' action, not a through action: that is, when bent to their test curve (tc) they do not form a curve of almost a semicircle, but instead the lowest two-thirds of the rod are more or less stiff and the curvature involves only the top third. The test curve I use is 1¾ to 2¼lb. It is necessary to have such a stiff action to set the hooks, which may be several trebles. Through-action rods have their place in angling, but not generally in spinning (for example, in fly fishing and deadbait fishing).

I'm emphasizing this issue because several manufacturers make a range of 'named' spinning rods, of different lengths, but the action may vary with the length. Usually, in such ranges it is the longer rods which have softer actions, so these are best avoided. If you do want a longer rod then search the ranges until you find a 10ft or 11ft rod that really will be fast/tippy enough for

Note that the reel to the right is incorrectly loaded, underfilled in fact, which would detract greatly from both distance and accuracy.

A big, round, 30in diameter landing net, superb for bank lure fishing, dwarfs this big twenty pounder.

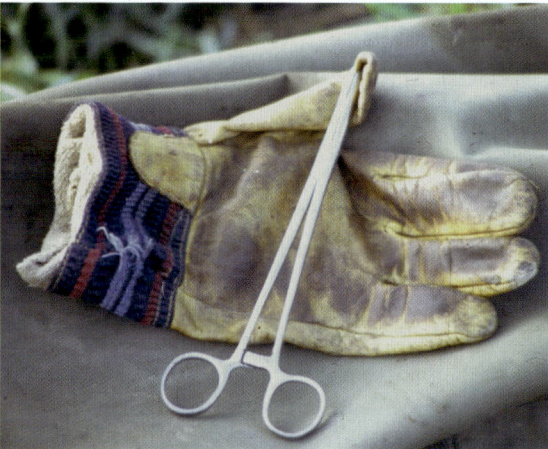

Glove and forceps for unhooking. In general, pliers are better for lure fishing.

spinning. Often enough the 9ft length in the range is the one most suitable for the pike angler. I'm not going to get involved at this point in the long versus short rod debate, because that will pan out logically in the following text, as you will see. Suffice it to say that a long rod (for example, 9ft) is always better for dealing with bankside growth, whereas a short rod is often advantageous on a boat.

My 9ft rod will be armed with a fixed spool reel. It is not necessary to use a giant fixed spool reel at all, and I usually choose one a size smaller than those used by pike anglers for bait fishing. If it takes 100m+ of 14–18lb bs line then that is fine. In terms of line I'm talking monofil in the last sentence, but if I'm on braid – and I like it and use it – I do not like thin braids. I'd choose 40lb braid over 20lb braid any day, although the latter is perfectly capable of landing the fish, obviously, because 14–18lb bs monofil will do the job. No, it's something to do with the very fineness of 20lb braid which doesn't feel right on the rod when I'm pike spinning. In terms of line colour, whether monofil or braid, I prefer dull or dark colours, such as brown or green, although clear monofil is fine so long as it is dull.

Of course, many anglers prefer to use multipliers even for the standard piking we are discussing here. There's nothing wrong with that. I often use them myself. The lines in use are the same, but the rod needs to be one with a butt section which allows the reel to be attached 'topside'. So if you want to switch from one reel to another on different days, you'll need two rods. I do this myself and for my multiplier I still use a 9ft rod. You can, of course, use the very same rod for both as long as the handle is parallel-sided cork, although a purpose-designed handle is more comfortable.

A lot of keen multiplier anglers go for shorter rods. You lose the advantage of

Trebles tangled in this kind of mesh (see text) can be extracted in seconds and hence the captured fish is not put at risk by delays, as happens with micromesh netting.

reach when bank fishing, but using a short rod, say down to 4ft or 5ft, when coupled with one of the small modern multipliers is a very pleasurable way of fishing and with lighter gear too. I've had 20lb pike on a rod as short as 4½ft, so this gear really will cope with big fish. I think the real drawback with the very short rods just mentioned is that when a big, fast pike goes on a run you just don't have quite the same control as with a 9ft rod, with which you can apply sidestrain much more easily. On a boat everything changes and the small rod is often much better, especially when a big fish nears the boat. When a big pike lunges beneath the boat, the short rod again has its limits. Essentially, it's what *you* prefer to do: long or short, fixed spool or multiplier. After a little experience, most pikers of my acquaintance do both.

Now we come to the question of what to do if you want to try some other fishing, perhaps smaller fish like perch, larger fish like salmon, or sea fishing for bass. Can you continue with the above tackle or do

you need to change? The answer is that you need to change. However, instead of going in for massive outlay financially – after all, you may already have a couple of rods and a couple of reels – you could use the 9ft pike rod for a few other ventures, just to see whether they are your cup of tea. I've done a lot of perch fishing with such a rod, as well as rock fishing for pollack and bass, and found that it was suitable for the sea fishing but a little heavy for the perch, so I changed to a 9ft rod with a test curve of 1¼lb. Such a rod would also do well for zander, because these do not grow as big as pike. Nor do they fight as hard, weight for weight. And it would be suitable for chub too.

Normally, I wouldn't use the short rod system for this kind of fishing unless it was from a boat. However, I'll relate a case when I fished a very small river in Cambridgeshire. It held plenty of perch and pike, but the latter were usually 2–5lb and the biggest I got was 10lb exactly. So I used a 7ft, very light rod (*see* Chapter 8) and a tiny fixed spool reel or equally tiny Ryobi multiplier and 6lb bs line. It was lovely fishing. On a few occasions, including on my lure fishing video (*Success with the Lure*; *see* Bibliography), I used the normal 9ft pike spinning rod. It seemed over the top to me, although it worked well enough. So personal choice and pleasure does come strongly into play in these matters.

Whilst our 9ft foot rod is fine fishing off the rocks for pollack, you would have to think again if you were beach-casting a plug, especially if the plug or lure was on a paternoster. I've found a 10ft or 11ft rod to be better and preferably one with a test curve of 2½b. In other words, you've stepped up a gear because beach fishing, or casting from one of those long, low promontories, really does need heavier gear to combat tide, currents and waves. Some would step up the gear a notch further, sacrificing (relative) lightness for a bit of extra power.

Snap-on leads for trolling, top left, and anti-kink leads. (Photograph courtesy of Gordon Burton)

You can see now where I'm going and why I took the 9ft pike rod as starting point: it's very versatile, but, eventually, you will need to change rod (and, perhaps, the reel) as you venture further afield than pike. There's one change I haven't mentioned yet because it is rather a dramatic one. I refer to jerkbait fishing or the fishing of large lures, be they crankbaits or big rubber jobs. The above pike rod is no good at all for this sort of fishing. You need a jerkbait rod, or two – I have two, one for use with a big fixed spool reel and one for use with multipliers. And lines need to go up to 60lb braid – it's a different world to most lure fishing.

If you took the standard pike lure rod salmon fishing, you might be okay on many waters. I've used mine on the River Wye, for example, and did not feel undergunned at all. But on some of the bigger, more turbulent or rocky waters you might need to think in terms of 10–12ft and more power, while remembering always the increased labour cost. Also in salmon fishing, multipliers are much favoured and some people go for rods with a slightly softer action than

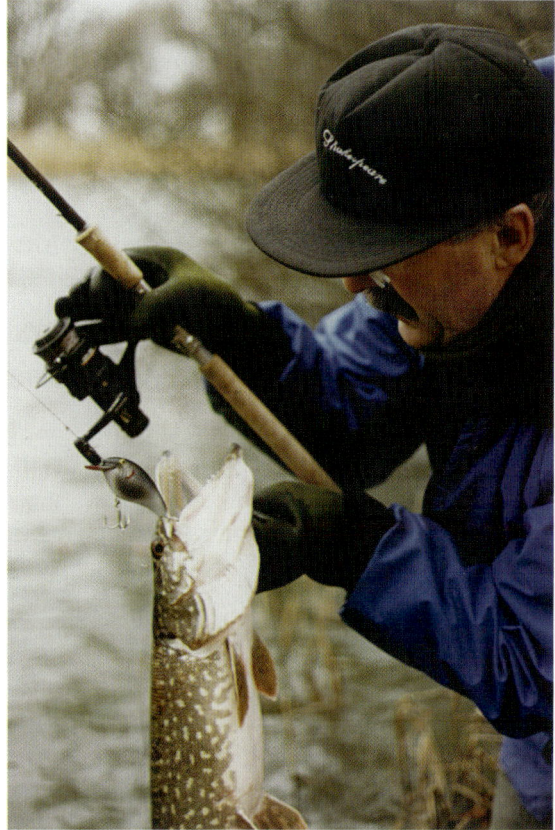

Winter lure fishing – gloves and warm clothes.

I have outlined above. For trout or sea trout spinning the normal 9ft pike rod is fine.

I'll not cover all the rod and reel eventualities, species by species, because fishing for different species is well covered in the rest of the book, but I will mention a little more about sea fishing from boats. A lot of sea boat fishing is done with jigs and perks, or other lures, often on a quite heavily weighted line. You need to take the boatman's advice or that of an experienced colleague, but basically you will be upping the rod strength to 20lb, 30lb class rods and more, plus they are usually relatively short. But boat fishing may also mean casting for bass or pollack and here it is probably better to use the upgraded bass rod that you might use from

35

the beach, as I outlined above – provided the boatman and your colleagues are happy about that because in the confines of a boat lures are flying everywhere!

Big game fishing is dealt with by David Bird (*see* Chapter 14) and this really is a different ball game – different rods, different reels. Fortunately, you can usually hire these from the boat hire people, although I prefer to have my own reel because so often the professionals have the multiplier handles on the wrong side. Big game fishing is not just about marlin, though. It includes tigerfish and Nile perch, for example. And here I have a deal of experience which tells me that from the bank you could manage quite well with a standard pike lure rod. I do prefer, however, a 3lb test curve rod, such as a 12ft pike rod, because Nile perch from the bank can exceed 100lb. My best is 120lb.

You can see, therefore, that we do have to move away from the one-rod-fits-all scheme of things as more and more different lure fishing is undertaken. If you do this in phases, rather than all at once, the expense is defrayed. I regard the rod as being more important than the reel. Choose the reel to match the rod if you can, but improvise if you can't. The line choice is usually fairly simple, as I have said (but *see* Gordon Burton's Chapter 7 for when more deliberation is needed). I'm not discussing end rigs in this chapter because all that will become clear in the appropriate places below.

Techniques

Particular techniques, clearly, will permeate the rest of the book. What I want to do here is to deal with the very basics, the things people often get wrong and which, therefore, detract from their enjoyment. In lure fishing in particular, one of the crucial starting points is to have the fixed spool reel

fully loaded with line. Underloading a spool seriously detracts from distances achieved, impairs accuracy and leads to bad casts and tangles, and yet one sees even quite experienced anglers with 5mm of spool rim showing before the cast is made. I load my spools to the very brim – after all, you'll have up to 15ft of line off the spool as you stand there ready to cast. I probably overload mine at times, but it is far easier to snip off 10yd than it is to add a length to an underfilled spool. With multipliers, it is slightly less crucial but a fully loaded spool gives you a better retrieve rate should you need it.

Left-hand-wind multipliers. The two right-hand rods are jerkbait rods, one for use with multipliers, one for fixed spool reels. Note the heavy braid on the fixed spool reel and the heavy monofil on the right-hand multiplier.

After watching a spinning man for a few minutes I can always tell if they are beginners or not, or whether they are unfamiliar with the water they are on. This is not so much to do with their manner of casting because my own style is nothing to brag about. It's to do with the manner of the retrieve of the lure. When I have been out with beginners they are often surprised at the number of takes, and fish I catch, in the swims where we are more or less fishing together. To a large part it is due to poor retrieve technique on their part. They cast just as far, but observe how often they get weeded up close in, or run into snags. As the lure hits the water you need to get it to its working depth as quickly as possible, while not hitting the bottom as this could foul up the lure in many instances, making that cast a total waste of time. After reaching the correct depth, the lure needs to be pulled in so that it more or less follows the contours, neither coming up nor going down unless you have a particular reason to do that. Equally, as the lure approaches the bank, often a deadly taking zone, the rod may need to be raised to bring the lure up the slope. A beginner will plough the lure into the bottom at this stage, thus missing out on the chance of a fish and perhaps spooking it at the same time. If you watch a beginner fishing like this you soon realize that their lure is effective only for about one-quarter of the cast distance, so, forgetting about all the other skills the experienced angler may also have, his cast is likely to be four times as productive as that of the inexperienced. This retrieve principle applies to all lure fishing and you can take it as read in the following chapters.

As noted above, close in is often a good taking zone. This is because fish often lurk there, using cover from which to attack, but also because fish may follow a lure some distance and only strike when they see their meal disappearing rapido. This last you can deal with by using a neat ploy. *Before* the lure gets into the bank zone, rise it in the water so that the predator thinks it is going to lose it. This can induce a strike and, what is more, it can induce a strike in a zone where the predator cannot see you – so if it misses the lure it may yet take it in the bank zone near the rod tip. I used this trick quite recently in Egypt to get several big Nile perch, but it works with many species. Naturally it can be used in boat fishing too, although fish rarely seem bothered by the presence of the boat itself.

What about the manner of the retrieve? In terms of speed of retrieve, we deal with that with regard to individual species later in the book, where it is appropriate but, for example, you might want to pull the lure back very slowly for pike in winter, but as fast as you can for trout. It varies a great deal. Usually it is best, at least to begin with, to retrieve the lure at the speed which seems to make it work best. All lures have an optimum action and the speed should be related to that. This implies a steady rate of retrieve and this is probably the best starting point in a swim. However, all anglers know that varying the action can help on many occasions, so it is a question of trial and error. If the steady retrieve, at optimum speed, fails to get results, try a stop–start approach, or speed it up, raise it in the water, sink it a little, and so on. Never get into a boring cast and steady retrieve if nothing is happening. Make it happen! And change lures until it does.

The actual approach of an angler to a swim can be crucial. Do not tread heavily. Sound, and that includes vibrations, travels nine times faster through water than elsewhere, so should you be heavy footed you'll certainly alert nearby fish, if not also those some distance away. There is a downside to pussyfooting it along the bank, in that you sometimes go head over heels in your efforts to be quiet, but it's a price worth paying. I know some anglers who are like elephants on the bankside. You can feel their footfalls. They simply don't get as many fish, especially close in and when bank fishing.

So approach a swim carefully, use cover and dress sensibly in dull or camo clothing. You can use cover behind you as well, such as a high bank or a reed bed, especially if the colour is a rough match to your clothes. In Egypt, the background 'cover' of rock is crucial because there are no bushes or reed beds to hide behind. One wears rock-coloured or dull outfits.

Stillness is another factor. Movement is what betrays prey *and* predator. If a fish is close in, or anticipated to be so, or is seen, then only move very slowly and what is absolutely necessary – the hands maybe, to cast. I have always found that the first few casts in a swim can be crucial, and also that it is possible to spook a fish by chucking a large lure at it. I know the opposite obtains on occasion and I do recall Fred J. Taylor recounting how he had to throw in half a brick on one occasion to get the pike on the move. Generally, though, I try a smaller, quieter lure to start with unless I'm very confident as to the taking lure at the time.

Finally, the little matter of casting systems and I can be brief about this. You will often read, and see explanatory diagrams, telling you to fish a swim quite systematically with a series of casts at 5-degree intervals – or something like that. I rarely, if ever, fish like this. On bad to poor days it can be excruciatingly boring and on good days it probably doesn't make an ounce of difference. Cast where you think the fish will be. That way, in time, you will learn the likely taking spots. I'll add one proviso. If I'm fairly sure that a particular part of a swim holds the fish I'm after, say under an overhanging tree, or in a hollow between weeds, then, instead of casting straight into its lair I'll make a few splashy casts some distance away from the lair, but close enough so that

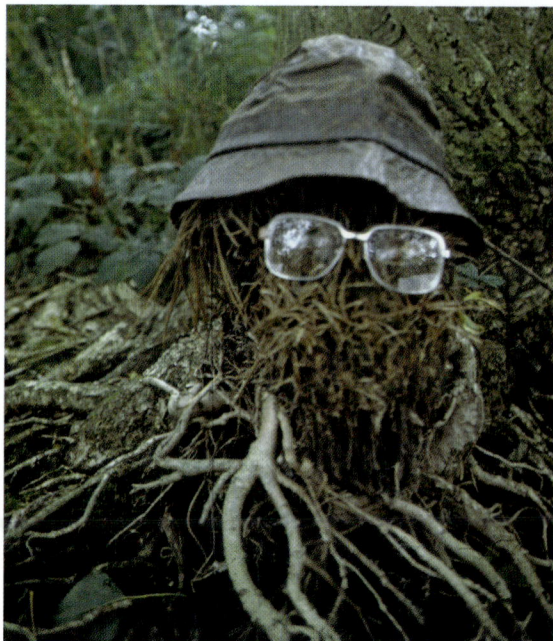

The ultimate in bank camouflage.

the fish hears the disturbance – say 20yd away. I'll even plop the lure up and down in the water at my feet, a bit like clonking for catfish! Then, having got the fish on edge, I chuck the lure right at it. This is often an excellent way of nailing a good fish.

All natural hunters are very careful, so take a leaf from their book. If you are a pike angler reading the foregoing you'll be thinking I have been writing for you. But I haven't. What I have done is cover the approach needed for all predatory fish in most situations. We all know that on occasion the predators will practically crawl up the bank, ignoring everything and everyone, but these are rare occasions; most of the time they need craft to catch them.

There is one last matter I haven't dealt with and that is the peripheral tackle that an angler might take with him on a lure fishing trip. I have deliberately left this until the next chapter, and from there it can be translated to fishing for other species.

3 Pike on Lures

In the past, many bait fishermen have been reluctant to take up lure fishing for pike, believing it only to catch small fish. Happily, that situation has changed and many anglers are catching big pike on lures. However, that is not the purpose, necessarily, of this chapter. What I say will help you to catch big pike, but it will also help you to catch any pike, full stop. I have another reason for writing about pike at this stage: it is a very good way to get into lure fishing. A few pike under your belt and you realize you could go on and catch other species, and it is true that game fishermen who fancy doing something other than fly fishing seem to take to lure fishing quite well, so this is for them too. Lure angling for pike can be a very specialist business too, as can all facets of the sport, and some of these more advanced matters are dealt with in Chapter 4, 5 and 7, although the principles set out by James Holgate in Chapter 4 and Gordon Burton in Chapter 7 also apply to many other fish, witness Gordon's ferox trout. Mostly in this chapter I want to get the basics of pike lure fishing correct, because from that so much else in lure fishing will flow.

How to get started? And where? I'll take the second of these first. The important thing is to catch a few pike. Whereas the experienced piker never bothers about the

A cheerful Gordon Burton, himself a true believer, with a nice pike on a Believer, on the troll. (Photograph courtesy of Gordon Burton)

Barrie practising what he preaches, fishing a surface plastic frog in lily beds to tempt a pike.

odd blank or three, the newcomer will get discouraged if some results are not forthcoming: they need to know that it works. My firm advice is to find a small river, even a very small river (as in my video, *Success with the Lure*; *see* Bibliography) or a canal. Small rivers often have plenty of pike in them and, what is more, their holts are usually fairly obvious, such as a deep eddy under a tree or undercut bank. Historically, canal pike have often been persecuted and sometimes still are. As a result, many canals have

a good head – or a bad head if you prefer – of small pike to be caught. If you are near any of the Fenland drains in Lincolnshire, Cambridgeshire, Somerset or elsewhere, seek out a small, relatively unfished one and you'll soon find plenty of pike. But my favourite type of venue, which I recommend above all, is the kind of shallow lake that is weed-covered in summer. In late autumn as the weeds die, such lakes can be superb for pike. These may be small pike, but it's pike we are after here, regardless of size.

Gordon Burton with a 20¾lb pike on Baby Depth Raider fished at over 60ft down. (Photograph courtesy of Gordon Burton)

The tackle you need to get started, in terms of rod and reel, was outlined in Chapter 2. Get a 9ft rod with a stiff action and begin with a fixed spool reel rather than a multiplier. Then we need to look at the rest of the gear that will be required. Some of it is quite vital. First of all, you need a wire trace with a swivel on one end and a link swivel on the other to which you attach the lure. *You cannot fish for pike without a wire trace.* Fortunately there are many good wires on the market, so I'll not recommend particular brands, but go for a breaking strain of 20–25lb. These are not thick wires, unlike in the past. You can buy made-up traces ready to go – I like the black, plastic-coated ones myself – but the link swivels on them tend to be a bit on the weak side. The trace must be no shorter than 12in because a big pike can completely engulf a lure and a 6in trace. Most lure fishermen make their own traces, simply buying big spools of various wires and boxes of swivels. You can manage without ball-bearing swivels, which are expensive; a lot of serious lure anglers use them, but not so many pikers.

Before you cast, you will need a few other items. Most anglers in freshwater game or coarse will be used to using artery forceps to remove hooks. These do not work well in lure fishing. The hooks are often bigger than in other comparable fishing, so you need something powerful enough to grip them firmly. I use long-nosed pliers and, fortunately, these are sold by several tackle companies and fit the bill well. You can also buy a tool called a hook-out, which is not dissimilar to pliers; these are excellent, if more expensive. However, there is another problem with lure hooks in that they occasionally hook a pike in such a manner that they are difficult to remove quickly. Rather than messing about and perhaps putting the pike at risk you need a pair of wire cutters to cut the hooks to bits. Again, these are on the market for pike anglers as hook snippers. After all, a treble hook is an easily replaced item and relatively cheap.

Another item you need is a left-hand glove (if you are right-handed). This enables you to hold the pike by its jaw with the left hand whilst you remove the hooks with the right

Muddy, cold, winter lure fishing, but this garish lure produced the goods.

Malcolm Bannister with a good Lake District pike.

hand. The gloves I like are soft, thick leather gardening gloves (usually bright yellow for some reason), but anything thick enough to prevent the teeth going too deeply into your hand will suffice. A little prick or two shouldn't matter, but carry antiseptic with you. I'll not go into detail of unhooking until I have discussed the next very crucial item, to whit the landing net.

Gaffs were banned in England several years ago; they were not very efficient in the first place. I began using landing nets back in the 1950s when most used gaffs, and nets really are better. They need to be big. If round-rimmed, which I prefer, they should be a minimum diameter of 30in; if triangular – that is, ex-carp nets – then the big ones on sale are obviously big enough. A friend made a net for me, but Fox does an excellent big, round net, with good netting. Netting is somewhat controversial, in that many pikers simply employ the same

nets that they use for carp in the summer. These nets are micromesh, which is good for many fish, but very bad for pike fishing. If you have a plug with trebles not in the mouth of a pike you have landed, that is, part hanging free, if the trebles get into the micromesh they are the devil to remove. I use a net material with a larger mesh, from Cabelas in Nebraska, USA, but the Fox net material is probably better. The barbed trebles are reasonably easily removed from both types, although the American net needs softening before use (when I have a new one I leave it on the drive in all weathers and drive the car back and forth over it for some weeks, after boiling it first; you don't need to do this with the Fox net).

I'm emphasizing this matter because if you get it wrong, the pike suffers. Some anglers, rather than risk a flying treble in the micromesh, decide to hand-land the fish. Although practised by quite a few

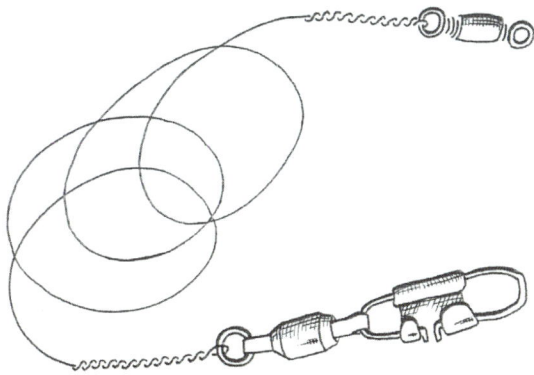

Pike wire traces are essential where any toothing prey is present. The upper swivel can be a ball-bearing swivel and the link swivel can be a safety pin type, like this, or cross lock for bigger game than pike.

Some of Barrie's favourite Fenland pike lures. The Creek Chub Pikie at the top has produced many big fish, while the red lure at the bottom often out fishes other colours.

experienced anglers, hand-landing is not a good idea, especially when trebles are flying loose. Other anglers fish barbless trebles to avoid serious tangling in the micromesh: this is really bad thinking. You use hooks to catch fish, not because they are easy to remove from net material, or from the fish for that matter. In any case, there is an increasing body of thought that barbless hooks, far from being kind to fish, are actually more damaging. Pike, in particular, are at risk from hooks which penetrate too deeply, because their heart is close to the top of the throat, on the under or ventral side. Barbless hooks penetrate more deeply and can move in position or become unhooked during the fight more easily than hooks with microbarbs or slightly pressed-down barbs. Microbarbs are all that are needed in piking. Barbless hooks on plugs are useless in my view. I have tried them extensively as far back as the 1950s and since. In fact, barbless hooks for big fish of any species would be best abandoned. Barbed hooks often penetrate just over the barb and not much further. In lure fishing the penetration can be deeper, but it only goes in once and deep-hooked fish tend to be a rarity. I haven't had one since 2002 and I've had some big fish in that time on lures.

So now we have a decent rod and reel, a decent landing net and some unhooking gear. We also need a backpack of some sort. Most use a small rucksack or shoulder bag. I'm talking bank fishing still, because on a boat you can take the kitchen sink. Your backpack will need to carry other items: food, drink, camera perhaps, a waterproof *and the lures*. The last raises another problem. I noted above that you need a decent number even for half a day's fishing, say thirty. On the bank you don't want one of those lure boxes. They weigh a ton and lugging them about simply discourages

Perhaps the best standby of all baits, the shallow-diving plug or crankbait, used either singly or in tandem.

you from exploring as you should. I'm still trying to persuade manufacturers to make a roll-up lure bag in which the lures do not tangle; the boss of Mepps Europe was keen at one stage but his team couldn't see the logic. So I carry mine in a cheap plastic bucket, in a jumble, but you'll be surprised how easy it is to untangle your lures. Simply lift all the lures up in one swift movement, grasp the one you want and let the rest fall back into the bucket. Your chosen lure, you will find, will be attached to a couple of trebles and easily removed. Actually I keep my unhooking gear, glove and spring balance in the bucket too.

Now we are ready to tackle that small water I mentioned earlier. I'm assuming that you'll be wearing clothing which does not give away your presence to the fish and that you'll tread lightly. You'll hunt. And that you'll practise some of the techniques outlined in Chapter 2. But I need now to say something about the choice of lures, because this is what will go through your mind as you stand there: where on Earth do I begin? If you haven't already got used

Surface poppers of all sizes work well in warmer months.

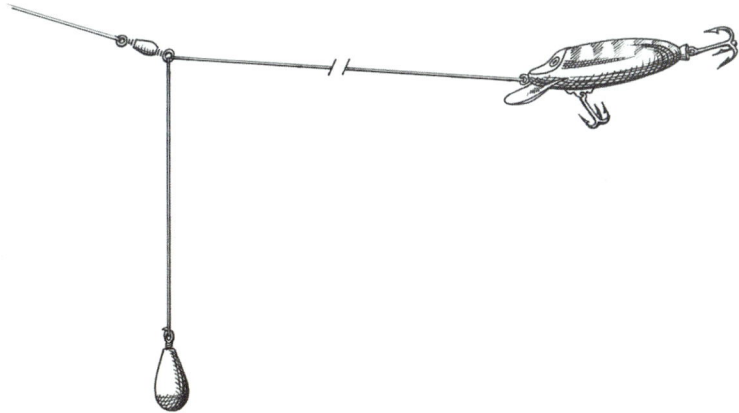

A good ploy on deep waters is to fish a paternostered floating plug (crankbait). The lead kicks up a 'dust' trail and the links can be set to ensure that the lure does not plough into the bottom.

to the water, I'd suggest beginning with a small crankbait like a Big S. The advantage of such a lure – and there are many to choose from – is that they float. What this means is that the beginner, not to mention me occasionally, can get his house in order before retrieving – make sure there are no loops on the rod, that the line on the water lies well and that the lure is in the right place. Once you are used to a fishery or a swim, you can switch to sinking lures if you think it's worth a shot. But begin with a Big S (or a Middy S if you might initially feel intimidated by the larger lure). The Big S goes down to about 3ft or so on a moderate cast, quite steeply too, but pops up easily if you think it's heading for a snag. You can easily search out all the crooks and crannies on a small water. It really is a top-class lure, with a long pedigree – you'll catch fish with it if they are there. The advantage of trying a small river is, of course, that you can fish it in summer when the pike are generally more active to lures. In contrast, shallow lakes and Fenland drains tend to get clogged with weed in summer, with the result that floating lures or small jigs are often your only option.

I want to digress briefly now, because I have just mentioned summer fishing. This

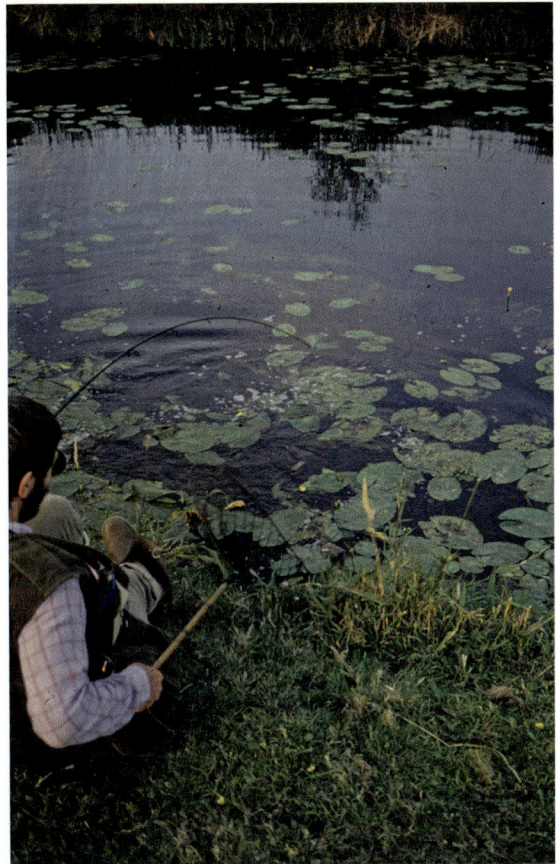

Bruce Vaughan playing a fish which took a surface popper.

45

is mildly controversial in two senses: one is that piking has traditionally begun in October; the second is that some anglers feel summer lure fishing puts the pike at risk. I do not think the second is true if you use strong gear, as outlined above, but, more importantly perhaps, also play the fish hard and quickly to the net. I have done thousands of hours of summer lure fishing and have no evidence from my own fishing that I'm doing any harm. On the contrary, the big fish I have caught in summer have been happily chomping baits in winter. So do it properly, with all the right gear, and it will be fine. On the bank with a fish do *not* spend ages photographing it. Take a quick picture and back in the water with it.

The next stage in piking is to get to know the water you are fishing, gradually trying new lures and new spots. On the shallow lakes which are weeded in summer I like to catch them when the weed is half died down and there's a bit of clear water above it. The time of year obviously varies with the weather patterns, but generally this point is reached in October. The first thing I do is put a mackerel spinner through the swims. It's an inconspicuous little fellow – to us – but it pulls the pike out of their holes in the weed. The problem is that when the weed is half gone you cannot do a long cast with even a shallow-diving crankbait because it's going to plough into a dying weed mass at some stage; also, the pike are just going 'off' surface-worked lures. I often use a lure beneath a 'float' (it is called a former) set at a depth such that it cannot foul up in a weed. If the former and the lure are heavy you can chuck them a long way.

By adopting these approaches you'll get plenty of pike, not always big ones but you'll gain confidence in your gear and techniques, especially if you can fit in some summer fishing and learn how to unhook lure-caught fish and return them safely. A last point in connection with this early phase of pike luring – if you are confined to winter fishing be ready for it to be slower, forget surface baits entirely and prepare to keep warm. You will often read that walking the banks while lure fishing in winter keeps you warm. It most certainly does not. The *walking* keeps you warm; stopping to cast can chill you to the bone in fifteen minutes. In winter, therefore, I fish for short periods only. I wear gloves. I fish a water with my back to the wind; if the wind is along the water course then I start fishing going with the wind and walk home into it. If it's seriously cold, I fish for fifteen minutes only, then sit down in the shelter and warmth and have a coffee. I have had some of my best lure catches in winter – indeed my biggest ever pike catch

Tim Cole with a tiddly summer pike on lure. Pike of all sizes are generally more active in summer.

The bronze hand of our artist Rebecca Lyne's famous sculpture 'Tick Man', refusing to release some of Barrie's favourite pike lures.

was on lures in winter – but the sport is slower generally and there is no getting away from that. Lure fishing in winter can be used in conjunction with bait fishing. If the pike are taking baits then you know they are there, which is a help. If they don't take the lures, they are often drawn in by them and then take the baits, so we are winners all round.

Once the would-be lure angler has gone through this initial phase, and I do strongly recommend it as confidence booster, he can start thinking bigger. Bigger waters

Big pike spoon (Lucky Strike Lizard) and small zander.

often have bigger fish, but they can be much slower in producing fish than the foregoing smaller waters. So mentally prepare yourself for this. Of course, you can speed up the learning process by going lure fishing with an experienced lure angler. This works, but it is still slower in terms of fish and he may outfish you a lot simply because of his knowledge; that can be hard. The great advantage of big-water fishing is that it will open up far more varied techniques to you. You can use big spoons and cast to the horizon. If the bottom is clean you can bump it with a spinnerbait or a Bulldawg, and so on. In short, you can use all the techniques outlined in Chapter 2.

You can use boats sometimes. This now takes us to the last phase, which is thoroughly dealt with in the following chapters: James Holgate will take you boat fishing; I will tell you all about jerkbait fishing; and then return to the specialist subject of rubber lures and jigs to add to the armoury. Remember, also, that these next chapters are not just about pike – the principles established within them will enable you to go out and tackle other species, coarse or game, freshwater or sea.

4 Boats and Big Waters

By James Holgate

Whilst interest in lure fishing has risen significantly over the past few years, I think it is fair to say that this surge has coincided with a significant increase in the number of pike anglers successfully getting to grips with larger than average lakes, lochs, loughs and other big deep venues.

There are several reasons for this, not least the increasing willingness of a greater percentage of pike anglers to invest in suitably large and well-equipped boats. Precisely how many pike anglers now regularly fish from a boat is difficult to assess, but it has certainly risen quite dramatically in the last few years. When I first set up the magazine, *Pike and Predators*, it was rare indeed to feature an article on fishing from boats; nowadays it is even rarer *not* to have a significant section of the magazine about pike fishing afloat.

The increased availability of high-spec accurate fish finders (echo sounders) has also helped in enabling more pike anglers to come to terms with big enigmatic venues, by helping them to reveal depths, contours and even, on occasions, their actual quarry. However, I think a third element is undoubtedly the fact that we are now seeing a much greater availability of lures suitable for tackling these big waters, along with a greater willingness of pike anglers to use lures of a size that would once have been considered way 'over the top' by our not so distant pike-fishing ancestors. Personally, I do not think the importance of this latter point can be over-estimated. I'm old enough to remember a time when pike anglers considered a 3in plug to be a 'large' bait, ignoring the fact that they would routinely use dead and live

The modern boat – a far cry from leaking, clinker-built, heavy wooden boats. (Photograph courtesy of James Holgate)

baits much bigger than that. Nowadays, of course, it is quite common for anglers fishing on large waters to be fishing with lures in the 10in and even 12in range. It is probably too glib to say that a lure should match the size of the water you are fishing, but it is, I believe, certainly a factor in the success modern anglers have enjoyed with lures on larger waters. Big lures tend to produce a correspondingly bigger 'signal' to the pike, enabling them to be drawn to the bait far more readily. Yes, it is true that this factor is not the be all and end all of lure selection, and it is possible to catch pike on any size of lure. However, lure fishing large waters tends to be about putting the odds as much as possible in your favour.

At the best of times, lure fishing a big, deep water can be a bit like searching for the proverbial needle in the haystack, but using a small lure of, say, 3in or 4in on such a venue is a bit like cutting that needle in half and then painting it the same colour as the hay!

Boats

A chapter about fishing lures from boats on large open waters would not be complete without a mention of the type of boat you should be looking to use on such waters. This is especially the case when it comes to lure fishing, because the traditional 'rowing boat' type design really can handicap you when casting lures. Although there really is no such thing as the perfect pike boat, let us nonetheless take a careful look at some of the points you should be considering.

For most practical purposes, a length of 12ft should be the minimum that most pike anglers should consider for anything but the smallest waters. A 12ft boat, if designed well, will provide a reasonable amount of space for two fairly organized pike anglers to fish from with a fair degree of efficiency. However, there are limitations on where I would personally be prepared to fish with such a boat. In my early days, I did very successfully fish from such a boat, even in quite large open waters, but in hindsight

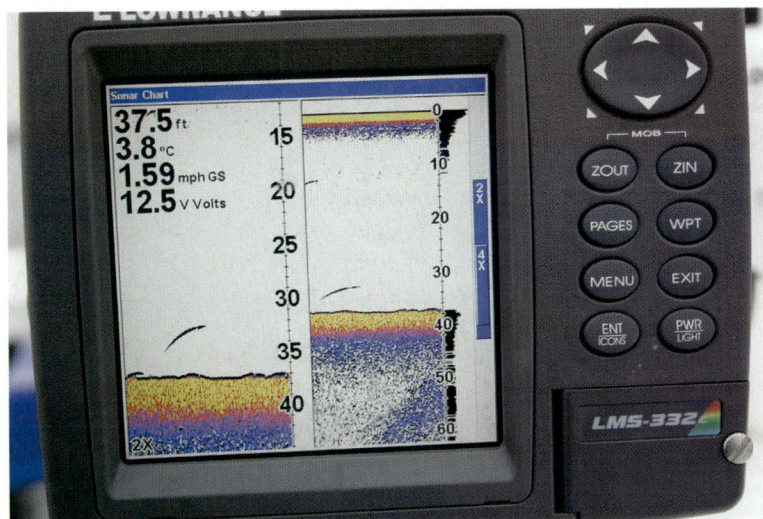

Echo sounders, a vital piece of gear for anyone afloat. (Photograph courtesy of James Holgate)

perhaps its size proved to have more limitations than I was prepared to concede at the time. I have to admit that I often I fished in conditions that were a little risky to say the least, and at times downright frightening. Therefore, whilst a 12ft boat is adequate in many situations, ranging from small to medium rivers, anything above a moderately sized reasonably sheltered still water and you will start to feel the limitations of such a craft.

Obviously, the issue is not about length as much as it is about freeboard – the amount of space between the surface of the water and the gunnels. I realize this is a very crude general principle, arising from a quite complex subject, but generally speaking the longer the boat the greater the freeboard and the greater the ability that boat has to ride waves and swell effectively. Having said that, I do realize there are some pike anglers who habitually use craft of 12ft on the largest waters that the British Isles has to offer; all I can say is, rather you than me! For anyone who is thinking of buying a pike boat, which is most often going to be used by two anglers at once, that will be suitable for all types of water, in a great variety of conditions without compromising safety, then I really don't think you should be looking at any craft under 14ft in length.

Obviously there is a cost issue involved here, which is that, unless you are very lucky and find a real bargain, the bigger the boat, the bigger will be the financial outlay. But I don't think it is any coincidence that the vast majority of pike anglers I have encountered who bought a boat under 14ft almost invariably want to sell it shortly afterwards for something larger. If cost is an issue in your decision to buy a small pike boat, then I would urge you to have a long, hard look at where and in what situation you are going to use such a boat. Moreover, if you feel you would really need something a little larger, then wait a while to save enough money to buy something larger. In most situations, this is probably the most economical course to take in the end. Put simply, a larger boat will be more versatile and less limiting that a smaller boat and you may be less likely to want to flog it at a loss a few months down the line.

We now come to the vexed decision of what design of craft you should be looking

Barrie's boat. At 12ft, a bit small.

for, a subject that all too readily illustrates the point I am making about there being no such thing as a perfect pike boat. Although there are a myriad designs of hull out there on the market, the best I can do here to bring some kind of order is to look at the most common and popular types of hull and examine their good and bad points.

Displacement Hull

One of the most common types of displacement-hulled boats used for pike fishing in this country is the Orkney. As the name suggests, this hull is so designed that when moving through water the front will 'displace' or 'push away' and small waves will appear at the bow and further aft along the hull. When speed is increased, these waves grow larger and the distance between them increases, until the boat is riding *between* the two waves that it is creating. At this point, the boat will be travelling at its maximum speed, so adding a larger engine will not make it travel significantly faster. Although safe and comfortable to fish from, this limit on the speed that can be obtained in such a boat can obviously be a drawback. It depends on the nature of your pike fishing and the waters in which you fish whether such a boat would be of use to you. Where speed is not a major requirement, such as on smallish waters or venues with low speed limits, then a displacement hull is a perfectly acceptable design.

Planing Hull

This type of hull design is also often referred to as a 'deep V' or 'semi V'. Again, the name provides a clue as to what this type of hull is designed for. Whilst the displacement hull pushes water, the planing hull, once it has reached sufficient speed to rise onto the plane, is designed literally to skim over the waves. As a result, much greater speeds can be achieved, and the bigger the

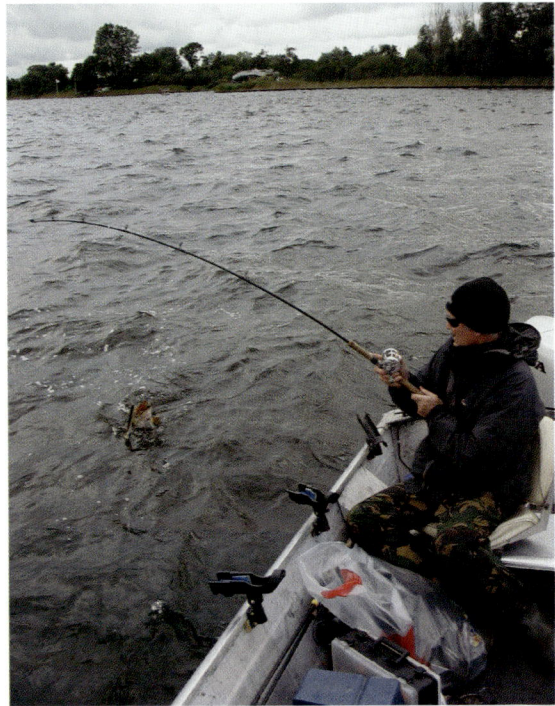

Action; and note the modern boat rod holders. (Photograph courtesy of James Holgate)

capacity of engine used, the faster the boat will travel (within the manufacturer's recommended limitations, to which I would strongly advise you to adhere).

Clearly, a planing hull will be of greater use to any pike angler where speed is going to be major factor on the waters they are fishing. They also make good trolling boats and are of benefit where casting lures and drifting is going to be widely practised.

Cathedral Hull

The oddly named cathedral-hulled boats are quite distinctive in design. Technically, most of the boats available are semi-cathedral hulls, but the design principle is pretty much the same. A (semi) cathedral-hulled boat is designed with three keels. In the case of the semi version, these consist of one main keel and two smaller keels at either side of the boat. Two of the most popular semi-cathedral-hulled boats are the Sea Hog and the Wilson Flyer, but there are several others.

The principal advantages of this type of boat are that it is very stable and will cope with even very rough conditions, while also containing a great deal of internal space. As the hull will lift on a plane, like the afore-mentioned planing hulls, it will also take a big engine and travel fast.

The main disadvantage of such a hull design is that, in my experience, it is not so good for trolling. In addition, in rough weather you tend to get wetter when travelling through waves than is the case with other boat designs, although buying a boat with a cabin can mitigate this. However, a fixed cabin is obviously not suitable for all styles of fishing.

Engines

I am assuming that most pike anglers buying a boat will require an engine of some sort, although obviously on small waters, or venues where engines are not allowed, you will have to revert to oar power. Buying the right type of engine to match the boat you are using, the venues you are fishing and your style of fishing is every bit as important as making the right decision when buying the boat itself.

There are several aspects of outboard engines to consider, but perhaps the most crucial will be engine size. Given that the choice available for practical pike-fishing purposes ranges from 4hp to models of 30+hp, there is as much potential to make the wrong choice as when choosing the boat. In addition, like boats, I suspect many first-time buyers will opt for engines that will be too small for their purpose.

The important point in favour of a larger engine is that, in my view, it is more versatile than a small engine. Put simply, a good, well-serviced engine of, say, 25hp can be made to travel as slow as you need for most practical purposes; on the other hand, there is obviously a limit on the speed you can get out of a smaller engine when you want to travel fast from one swim to another on a larger water. Notwithstanding speed limits that exist on some waters, pootling around on a large water with a 5hp outboard may seriously cut into your actual fishing time, because you may end up spending a substantial amount of your time simply travelling from one swim to another.

Of course, if you are only ever going to pike-fish on small waters where you don't need to travel large distances, then the smaller engine will be the best option, especially if there are difficult issues with launching your boat. In such a scenario, it may be preferable to buy an engine you can easily carry in your car and fit once the boat has been launched down, say, a steep bank. Anything over about 6hp is simply going to be too heavy to do this safely.

Sometimes it may be better to opt for a compromise in engine size, and certainly something around 15hp will stand you in good stead on many waters.

Another question you will need to ask yourself with regard to engine choice is whether to opt for steering by tiller or by remote, the latter being steered by a wheel located on a column positioned in the boat. Having used both, I can honestly say that your choice once again depends largely on the type of pike fishing you intend to do. If you are a pike angler who tends to fish statically – driving to a swim, anchoring up and fishing baits – then a remote steering system will be perfectly okay. On the other hand, if you are at all a more active type of angler, especially if you prefer to troll baits, then I would err on the side of tiller control. In my experience, tiller

Proof of James' pudding. (Photography courtesy of James Holgate)

controls are substantially more responsive and therefore much better at undertaking the twists and turns that are often necessary in many forms of trolling. You can get around this by fitting a smaller-powered extra auxiliary engine with a tiller control, with the main engine being remotely controlled, and using the auxiliary engine for trolling. I have done this successfully on many boats and it is certainly a viable option.

The last choice you need to make with regard to petrol engines is whether to opt for a two-stroke or four-stroke model. In future years the choice will not be as complicated because two-strokes are being phased out of the market, with some major manufacturers, such as Honda, now only producing four-stroke engines. Yet, there are still some cracking and very economical two-stroke engines out there, both second-hand and new, so the choice is still to be made. Let us first look at some of the pros and cons of four-strokes:

Pros

- quiet and smooth operation
- good fuel economy
- no need to bother mixing petrol and oil
- less pollution and smoke
- excellent at slower idling speeds for trolling, and so on.

Cons

- much heavier than two-strokes
- twice as many moving parts with potential to go wrong
- generally regarded as being less powerful for a given horse power
- greater cost.

For two-strokes, the pros and cons are as follows:

Pros

- two-strokes are significantly lighter than the equivalent horse-powered four strokes

53

- faster acceleration
- less expensive to buy
- simple design, meaning fewer things to go wrong and possibly easier servicing.

Cons

- need to mix petrol and oil together
- two-strokes are, allegedly, being phased out and some waters may even ban their use in future, although, generally in this country, such a prohibitions on petrol outboards usually don't make a distinction between the two types of engine
- two-strokes are generally noisier than four-strokes
- more smoke and pollution.

A bit to think about there! Overall, I would tentatively suggest that if you can afford it go for the four-stroke. If price is a problem then the two-stroke, despite its limitations, might be a better option. Moreover, there certainly is a big difference in cost, as you will see when you price up the different types of engine.

As with so many issues involved in choosing a boat, there is clearly no completely unambiguous answer to the question of which engine is best for your style of fishing, just a series of choices based on the kind of pike fishing you envisage. As it is obviously easy to make an expensive mistake, hopefully what I have said here will provide you with some of the questions you will need to ask about your own pike fishing in order to come up with suitable answers.

Internal Layout

The subject of how the boat should be laid out internally will very much depend upon your intended style of pike fishing. Thankfully, the days are long gone when pike

anglers had to settle for an internal design that was essentially just a rowing boat fitted with rows of wooden bench seats, which entailed doing to hurdles over them in order to travel from one end of the boat to the other. Certainly, if you were considering buying a boat with seats like this, I would think long and hard before choosing to do so. At least consider whether you will be able to remove some of those seats without compromising the structural integrity of the hull, replacing them with pedestal seats. This not only makes for fishing that is more comfortable when you are trolling lure, but the extra floor space really can be a boon.

With regard to lure fishing from boats, there is one feature you should seriously consider adding to your boat, and that is some form of raised casting deck. I have heard very reputable lure anglers say they can get along perfectly well without such an addition to their boat. Some prefer instead to use the plank seats to stand upon when casting and retrieving their lure. However, if you intend to do a lot of cast and retrieve lure fishing from your boat, then I really cannot stress how much easier it is to do so from a raised casting deck.

Again, whether you want to go to the expense or trouble of finding a boat with a good casting deck fore and aft really depends upon how much lure fishing you intend to do, but I think it is true that having a casting deck on your boat makes it highly likely you will lure fish for longer. When lure fishing from such a deck, you will find it both easier to cast (and that little bit further) and to control the lure, especially when employing such methods as jerkbaiting.

True, pike anglers can and do catch pike on lures from boats that are not only without casting decks, but also possess large bulky cabins to add to the difficulties. However, frankly I suspect most

A selection of trolling lures for big waters. (Photograph courtesy of Gordon Burton)

anglers who do this will still primarily be bait-and-wait type anglers. Nothing wrong with that, of course; I adopt that approach myself as and when I feel the situation requires. As I have tried to stress throughout this chapter, there really is no such thing as a perfect pike-fishing boat – only by asking long, hard questions about the type of boat you require for your own style of fishing will you be able to avoid a lot of expensive mistakes, in an area of pike fishing that can be something of a money pit at the best of times.

Talking of money brings me to another item of equipment almost equally vital for the modern lure angler fishing from a boat on any reasonably large water – the decent fish finder. I stress the word 'decent' because in my view a lot of anglers don't get the best out of their finders for the simple reason that they don't pay nearly as much attention to them as they should. The amount of information that a fish finder can reveal about a big lake to the thoughtful angler can be vital. Yet, so many give the screen only the occasional cursory glance; they get a rough idea of the depth but do not really use the finder to get a more detailed picture of the area they are fishing. I could probably be accused of being slightly obsessive about finders, but I really do think if taken notice of they can reveal details about the nature of the lakebed that will, on those difficult, dour days in particular, make the difference between catching and blanking. This is especially true when it comes to spotting those smaller, less noticeable features that can hold a few pike, but which tend to be overlooked by many pike anglers.

These days, on most waters in the UK, most well-equipped pike anglers will have a reasonable knowledge of the general contours of a lake and the big features, which everyone then concentrates upon. So using the finder to get a better working knowledge of those big features, and especially how they relate to other nearby features, is the key to greater consistency, as is knowing the whereabouts of those less noticeable features that can still throw up pike. However, you will only know where they are by paying close attention to the fish finder, which can only happen if the fish finder is in such a position that you can see it whilst you are lure fishing!

Trolling with Lures

Having now discussed the requirements, let us move on to the actual techniques for boat fishing on large waters. There are obviously two main methods of fishing lures from boats, these are trolling and cast and retrieve fishing. Anglers tend to separate these two methods, with many favouring one over the other. In my view, trolling and cast and retrieve fishing are simply two very vital parts of an overall approach to fishing on large waters; just as your left hand is an aid to your right hand, and vice versa, so these two techniques should not be viewed in isolation. Lure trolling, if carried out properly, can help you to find concentrations of fish, which you can then fully exploit using cast and retrieve methods far more quickly than can be achieved if you simply fished cast and retrieve all the time.

As I have just intimated, trolling has tended to be viewed as something of a lazy, no-brainer method, something to be done when all else has failed. Just chuck a couple of lures out the back of the boat, take your brain out and chug around the lake until a pike hangs itself on a lure. Admittedly, you can troll lures like this and, on occasion, you will be successful. Trolling does require a little less physical effort than standing up, casting and retrieving your lures all day long; most of the effort with trolling is mental rather than physical.

There are several factors you should concentrate upon when trolling, not least being the speed at which you troll. Again, modern GPS-equipped fish finders can help greatly in this respect, because they enable you to see the speed at which the boat is travelling with a great degree of accuracy. This is very different from the old days, when you had to estimate speeds, which can be quite a difficult feat, especially over water and in particular when there was any kind of flow or wind on the water. Trolling into the wind

on the same throttle setting would mean that the boat, and hence the lures, would be travelling significantly slower than when the boat was turned and fished in the direction of the flow. Now, with a GPS you can get your speed just right. What is more, you will notice that certain lures work best at certain speeds.

So, what kind of speeds are we talking about for lure trolling in most situations? As a rule, I would be looking at fishing lures anywhere between 1½–3mph. The type of lure I am using will to a certain extent govern the speed at which I travel when trolling. However, there are also other factors, not least being what I am hoping to achieve by trolling. That might sound like a strange consideration; after all, the point of trolling is to catch pike. The context can be important nonetheless. For example, if I am fishing a water that is fairly new to me, I will tend to choose lures that I know from experience can be trolled fairly fast. I do this because I am essentially using trolling as a searching method. If I can, say, fish lures as fast as possible, I can then find out about the water that much more quickly. The fish will reveal possible locations by being caught on the lures, or, failing that, at least I will be able to gain a good general impression of the water's underwater contours and possible pike holding areas that much more quickly.

On the other hand, on waters better known to me, I may choose lures that can be trolled more slowly, but, frankly, not that much more slowly. I sometimes use slower trolling methods as a kind of halfway house between full-blown trolling and cast and retrieve fishing. This technique works best on areas of water with quite extensive features, over which the pike tend to be more spread out. Alternatively, with a bit of forethought you can also arrange your trolling so that it takes in two or even three or more good potential features in one trolling pass, which in some circumstances can be a much more efficient way of covering several good areas in turn.

Lures for Trolling

As for the type of lures that work for trolling, my own personal preference is for either crankbaits or soft plastics. The characteristics all my trolling lures share is that they are fairly large. In the case of soft plastics, I rarely use lures smaller than 10in long, usually bigger. On occasion I do use crankbaits a little smaller, but nothing less than 8in. The main reason for using bigger baits is not, as has been suggested, some kind of macho thing, but because that is what I have found to be successful most of the time. It would be tempting to suggest that larger baits are more successful simply because they are more attractive to the larger pike and this should not be discounted. However, I suspect there is another reason and that is that large baits, either soft plastic or crankbaits, generally have the *potential* to get down that much deeper than their smaller counterparts. I stress the word potential, because, of course, it is not always necessary to fish your baits as deep as possible. Moreover, especially on clear waters, it can sometimes be a positive advantage to allow your lure to travel significantly higher in the water column, as pike will come up from the depths to intercept a bait. Put simply, because of the way a pike's vision works, it can sometimes spot a lure more easily further away than close to it.

For trolling, big lures are simply more versatile. By fishing your lures on varying degrees of shorter and longer lines, you can effectively control the depth at which they are travelling. Clearly, in the case of soft plastic baits that sink, you will need to fish them on a significantly longer line than you would a crankbait, which relies on getting down to depth on its diving vane. This is

A selection of Barrie's trolling lures. The top one is nearly a foot long.

why I often use both crankbaits and soft plastic at the same time, trolling the soft plastics some distance behind the boat and the crankbaits closer to the rear of the boat. I employ the different qualities of each type of lure to explore fully the entire spectrum of the water.

Hitting takes whilst trolling should not be a cause for panic. The main problem tends to be getting the rods out of the rests when they are under pressure from a taking pike in one direction and the forward momentum of the boat in the other! I wish I could say I have devised an easy technique for doing this, but often it is largely a question of using a bit of brute force to get the rod out of the rest and start playing the fish. Some rod rests are now available which are said to make this process easier, but until I use them myself, I cannot really comment on whether they are particularly effective.

You will obviously need to invest in good-quality *solid* rod rests that do not fall apart after a couple of season's abuse. The Berkley rests are just about okay, but as far as I am concerned, a company called Scotty makes the real daddies. They really will stand up to a lot of abuse and are well worth seeking out.

Of course, trolling is only part of the picture and when boat fishing is discussed, lure fishing tends to be divided into two distinct categories. The first is trolling, while the second is static fishing, when the boat is anchored and the lure angler uses the boat as a simple fishing platform, which I will discuss shortly. However, there is a third option, which could be described as a halfway house between these two extremes. I am, of course, referring to drifting.

Drifting with Lures

As the name suggests, drifting in its simplest form involves letting the boat drift unhindered around a water, using a flow or wind to move the boat over a number of swims. However, like trolling, drifting is an art in which, generally speaking, the more thought and effort you invest, the greater will be the rewards.

So, what kind of scenario favours drifting? I tend to regard drifting as a searching method that is a little more 'detailed' in its execution than trolling. It is especially useful in bodies of water where the pike are fairly widespread in a specific area, but *not tightly concentrated* over a particular feature. Shallow bays close to spawning time spring to mind, or just fairly featureless areas that for whatever reason seem to hold pockets of pike, but do not seem to be especially concentrated.

Having said that, though, it is still possible to drift and cast towards and over features. The beauty of lure fishing features like this is that it can enable you to present your lure in a variety of ways as you approach and pass over the drop-off, reef, depression or whatever you are fishing around.

The importance of this varying approach cannot be overestimated and often you will find that a lure presented on the feature at a particular angle will prove to be the one that trips the pike's trigger and makes it strike. Most of the time it is not possible to say with any certainty why a lure fished at a particular angle will work, but, believe me, it does! In addition, drift fishing really does help you to get to grips with many features in a more profound way than either trolling or just plonking down the anchor and hoping for the best.

Like most lure anglers who drift, I tend to cast *towards* the direction of the drift, rather than 'behind' – in short, casting towards where the boat is going rather than where it has been. To a certain extent this is because when I am fishing in this way I sometimes have a bait fishing out of the back of the boat. Having said that, however, this is not a strict rule and if I pass over what appears to be an interesting feature whilst drifting, I may well choose to start casting behind the boat back towards the feature, hopefully to give my lure the best chance of being in the right area. One point you should bear in mind when casting and drifting is that the direction in which you cast and retrieve will have a bearing on the lure's speed and hence its presentation. Put simply, if you are fishing your lures ahead of the drifting boat, the speed of the lure through the water will be slower for a given rate of retrieve than if you cast the same lure in the opposite direction. When the boat is drifting quite fast, this can have a profound effect on the depth at which your lure is being fished, as well as its action. Not always a vital factor, but worth thinking about, especially if your boat partner seems to be enjoying more success than you are! Like so much in lure fishing, it all hinges on thinking about what you are doing rather than just casting like a metronome.

Although it is possible in some reasonably benign conditions simply to cast and drift without much effort, in most situations you may have to employ some means not only to control the speed of your drift, but also the direction in which you are drifting. As far as speed is concerned, one vital item will be a drogue, as favoured by fly fishermen. When deployed properly, this item will help to slow your drift in conditions when the prevailing wind is pushing the boat too quickly.

Of course, a drogue can only slow your speed; it cannot alter your course, which is where an electric engine comes in. By far the best form of electric motor for this purpose is a bow-mounted motor. At the moment, I use an American engine, the Minn Kota PowerDrive, the speed and direction of which is controlled via a foot pedal or a remote control, not unlike a TV remote control. A slight touch on the foot pedal can help slightly alter your direction of drift and just generally keeps you on your preferred line.

However, I realize that this type of motor is not especially common in the UK at the moment and you are more likely to acquire a traditional transom-mounted engine. Fear not, I used one of these engines for cast and drift for many years and found it perfectly adequate, if not quite as versatile as the bow-mounted engine. You may find it helpful when using a transom-mounted engine to acquire an extension handle for the controls on your engine, so as to make it easier to use, but this really depends upon the design of your boat and the location of the engine in relation to your casting position.

Static Lure Fishing

I now come to my second-noted form of tackling a big water with lures from a boat. Frankly, anchoring up and fishing lures from a static boat is my *least* favourite form of lure fishing on a big water. However, even if you share my dislike, if you want to keep catching with lures on a big water, then you really cannot afford to ignore the method.

For me to anchor up and fish lures in such a static manner tends only to occur when the conditions are simply too wild

Big water (Lake Nasser, Egypt) and Martin Gay with a 90lb fish.

to consider either trolling or drifting. Even so, if I have to fish lures this way, then I will still try to do it right. Many pike anglers who fish this way tend to anchor up thoughtlessly and thus hamper their lure presentations.

The most common fault is either to fish too close or too far away from the main feature you want to fish. For example, if you are intending to fish lures over a drop-off, it is sometimes actually better to anchor your boat almost *on the* drop-off itself. This might seem like an odd thing to do, but by positioning your boat in this way you can run your lure *along* the drop-off on either side of the anchored boat, thus increasing the potential area where you will get takes. If you were to anchor your boat further away, you would only be able to run your lures across a far smaller portion of the potentially productive area. This is only one small example, but illustrates how important boat positioning can be. After all, unlike trolling or drifting, once you are anchored, you are pretty much committed to one area for a significant portion of your fishing session, so a few minutes getting your position just right to maximize your chances will be time well spent.

Of course, anchoring up needn't be the end of the matter, and if you were not experiencing any takes in your first chosen spot, then by all means get that anchor up and try another spot. How long to give each area? Well, personally, if I am getting no response from a variety of baits and presentations, in around half an hour I will have no hesitation in upping anchor and moving to another likely area. I do realize that some anglers, if they feel an area is worthwhile, will anchor up and keep casting the lures for the entire day and get good results. However, that is not my style; if nothing else, a change to another area will at least reanimate my hope and keep me casting with more conviction than if I stayed in the one area. That is not to say I would not consider a return later in the day to an area in which I had previously blanked. Swims can 'switch on' at different times and it never pays to write off a swim completely based on just one visit. Whether these swims switch on because pike have moved into the area, or the pike were there all the time and simply came on the feed during your return, is probably impossible to answer, but it is worthwhile noting when swims seem to produce their best results. If you are lucky and lure-fish the water often enough you may be able to find swims more likely to produce in the morning and others more likely to do so later in the day.

So there you have it, three very distinct techniques for fishing lures on big waters. However, none of these methods should be considered in isolation – they all work at the right place and the right time and often it is usual to employ all three techniques in differing degrees during the course of any one day out on the water. Given the fact that pike can be such disobliging creatures at the best of times, the fact that there is always something else to try, regardless of the conditions, is a factor in fishing big water that cannot be underestimated.

5 Jerkbait Fishing

It is necessary to deal with this subject separately, as it involves new tackle rather than modifications of the old, and also requires a new attitude of mind. Put crudely, it is a heavier, hard-working 'macho' style of fishing and it can be tiring too. The technique came to us from the USA, where it was, and is, in widespread use in muskie fishing. It was quickly put into use in the UK for pike fishing and has many advocates. But it is perhaps important to realize that the method has wider applications. I have already mentioned the big predators, muskellunge and pike, but I have also used it with some success for Nile perch and tigerfish in Egypt, and it works in sea fishing too. The miniature version of this aspect of the sport also works with smaller species, so there is real scope yet for experimentation.

Let's tackle first the new mindset which is needed. Most aspects of lure fishing have an element of the crafty hunter about them, of dexterity and quietness. Of course, even with jerkbaits you need to obscure yourself from the view of the prey and, as always, tread softly, but the comparison ends there. You really do need a line of 60–80lb braid, a short, powerful rod to match and reels man enough for constant heavy casting. I ought to say now that most of the top-class jerkbait anglers I know, such as Dave Lumb, Dave Kelbrick or Malcolm Bannister, use multipliers for jerkbait rods. They are certainly tougher reels for the job, the problem with fixed spool reels being that the pick-up, sooner or later, gives up the ghost if put to heavy and repetitive activity. Being a cussed soul I use both reels at different times. I have two identical rods, one which takes a multiplier and one which takes a fixed spool reel. Both will cast a 12oz lure. There are plenty of good jerkbait rods around – I use my two because I assisted in their development – and if you looked up Dave Lumb's website you'd soon find what you needed, or he could advise. The rods are much more powerful than the standard lure rods and even the normal 3lb tc dead-bait rods. Mind you, when I first started jerkbaiting at the instigation of Malcolm Bannister, I did use a 3lb tc bait rod quite successfully, but it is hard and tiring work even by jerkbaiting standards.

Now, why do we need such powerful lines? Clearly it is not to land the fish because in

The famous Hedgehog; classic jerkbait. Note the lack of any diving vane.

other kinds of piking, say, we'll be using monofil of 15–18lb. It's because you have to jerk the bait repeatedly in order to give it action. Unlike crankbaits, jerkbaits do not usually come with any kind of diving vane – in fact, one such would hinder the induced actions. The idea is to use the rod tip to jerk the bait so that it darts forwards, or slides sideways, or upwards, or downwards. Compared with crankbaits, it is an exaggerated retrieve pattern; often it looks like a dying fish which makes those final futile and uncontrolled darts sideways and upwards. A jerkbait roughly imitates this action. But jerkbaits are so varied that you can get all manner of actions and, as always, can vary the colours and the sizes. They don't just float. You can get sinkers as well. I have used sinking Salmos to catch both Nile perch and tigerfish, although the latter go for floaters as well. Salmos also work well for pike on the Fenland drains.

Now we come to the business end of the gear: the trace and the link swivel and trace swivel. It follows from all the foregoing that these need to be robust plus. Ordinary seven-strand wire isn't much good in my experience, because it kinks before long, or it curls up after a fish or two (mind you, I find it does that for bait fishing as well). So you need around 12in of stiff wire. The Ad Sweir traces I use for pike fly fishing are too short for this work, but the principle would work perfectly. I do use the black plastic-coated wire traces in the longer (commercial) lengths, but both the swivels and link swivels really do need replacing. Better still is to buy a spool of this wire and then you can make the traces yourself. It's lot cheaper and you get exactly what you need. Get either very strong swivels or ball-bearing swivels; what you pay for the latter you save on the bulk spooling of the wire. When it comes to the link swivels I always try to get cross-lock swivels of a size I have difficulty opening with my fingers.

If I struggle, then the fish will struggle to open them too. I find they are a little larger than the ones I choose for deadbaiting – and then I realized that it wasn't so much the fish that weakened the swivels but the repeated casting and jerking retrieve.

So it's all a bit different to 'lightweight' lure fishing. But, my word, it can be very effective. There is a problem, of course, and you may have spotted it by now. I said earlier on in the book that it was quite easy to spook pike by using a lure which is too heavy and splashy. This is true, and there is no easy answer to this one. Quite often I travel the banks carrying two rods, a standard lure rod and a jerkbait rod. But better still is to think jerkbaiting for the day. There are probably many reasons for the success of jerkbaits. One is certainly that UK pike haven't seen them before on many waters. I know waters in the Fenlands that haven't seen a jerkbait to this day, though they will do so before too long. Another, and perhaps more important, reason is that the jerkbait in its usual form represents, in the pike's mind, a really good feast. Big pike, given a choice, do prefer a sizeable food item. Indeed, they won't grow very well unless they get a few of them. There's yet another factor, which is that big pike are known to be very territorial and sometimes their response to a jerkbait in their baili-wick may simply be to see off the intruder. They might ignore small intruders – often do – but a big one is seen as more menacing. Anyone who doubts this territorial attitude of big pike should watch some of the underwater film clips of them. Therefore, for a whole host of reasons – newness, size, action, colours, very presence – jerkbaits pull big pike.

The use of jerkbaits tends to have been pioneered in this country in big waters, reservoirs especially. But it is important to recognize that they work in most places. One of my earliest experiences with them was on a small lake. The jerkbaits were about 10in long and weighed a ton. They hit the water like a plane crashing, but I had several pike on them in a couple of hours, the best 9lb. That raises another matter. On this particular lake, which holds pike to nearly 30lb, I have never had one over 10lb on jerkbaits. So you really have to try your waters. Do not be discouraged if they do not work on one water, try another. Or try another time.

Let us return now to the unique feature of jerkbaits, namely the actions you impart to them. It follows that the jerkbait does not have to be large. And in the UK, after several years of large jerkbaits flying through the air here, there and everywhere, some anglers began using small jerkbaits. Excellent ones are sold by Fox, for example, or you can make your own. As a digression it is worth mentioning that small to medium-sized jerkbaits can easily be made by taking the diving vanes off crankbaits. They do not always work but, as a rule, they do. Use of smaller jerkbaits does get around the spooking problem and they are easier on the arms. Of course, they also catch other fish such as perch and chub. You can now get jerkbait rods for smaller jerkbaits. I use one made by Shakespeare, but which is now out of production. However, it must be said that if you are using small jerkbaits you can revert to an ordinary pike lure rod, and I often do. I either concentrate on big jerkbaits, or take some smaller ones with me on an ordinary lure fishing day. It is still advisable to use heavyish braids, say 40–50lb bs because the jerk action will wear thin lines too quickly. I haven't advised on particular braids because it's very much a personal choice. I have used both the soft and hard braids, and on the whole prefer the latter because the soft ones do fray quite a bit after a season's use.

I haven't mentioned rod rings yet, but it must have occurred to you that they come

Rubber jerkbaits, which can be fished very slowly: on the left, surface big plugs; a Burmek on the right; and a surface popper-cum-buzzer. All these require rod action to work them.

under a bit of stress. They do. All the reputable manufacturers use high-quality rings on their jerkbait rods. You must have tough, well-lined end and butt rings. If you are making up your own blanks then ensure you take advice about seriously good rings.

It may also have occurred to you that lines of 60–80lb will take some breaking if you snag up irretrievably. In fact, this is rarely a problem unless you use sinking jerkbaits in snaggy waters. Surface-fished jerkbaits rarely snag up; if you chuck them into overhanging branches then a severe tug will usually release the lure plus a few twigs – or reeds, rushes or grass of the opposite bank! It is possible to marry the link swivel to the line in the sense that if you can get a link swivel that yields before the line breaks then at least you can 'free' the lure from the tackle. You can test the swivels beforehand when you buy a batch. Some have the straight-pull breaking strain marked on the packet, but test them anyway.

Some anglers get into tangles with braids, but this is not my own experience. In fact, I get far fewer tangles than with monofils. In jerkbait angling the matter is very important because the lure may be travelling like a Polaris missile and any sudden hold-ups (such as a loop going around a rod ring) will ensure that it continues to do so, but free of the reel line! The loop around the rod ring problem can be solved to a degree by smoother casting. And it is quite important to check the reel spool for sticking-out loops before casting: a glance is all that is needed. Again, it all points up the need for strong lines when jerkbaiting, simply because of the hard work they have to do.

So far, I've written as though the angler is bank fishing but on boats the principles are really very similar. You may not need to cast as far. You may be able to float a lure down the wind, or motor away from it, and get a really long, easy retrieve. In both boat and on the bank most retrieves will be with the rod tip pointing to the water, with the wrists used to, literally, jerk the bait, working the tip from side to side, up and down, occasionally giving it a slower glide, or a stationary spell – exactly like a prey fish in trouble, in fact. Give it life, or the remains of one. On a boat, the necessary short, powerful rods come into their own. On the bank, choose your casting position well and plan the position for landing the fish. You can, of course, troll jerkbaits, but this really does mean learning your lures. The troll speed needs to be carefully monitored, especially when a lure is changed – all is not well when the lure planes to the surface all the time, or, more particularly, planes along the surface. You can still catch fish, of course, because a predator will take a dying fish off the top in warmer conditions.

I have deliberately left until this point the matter of how to use a multiplier reel. Fortunately, so many anglers use them these days that they are not seen as being so off-putting as they were when I was young. Almost all modern multipliers come with an efficient centrifugal braking system, often with the numbers 1–10 on it. When using a new reel, or after a lay off of some weeks, I unashamedly start with a high brake setting, even number 10. This means that I'll get no overruns at all, even though the cast distance is cut. Then, as I familiarize myself with the reel, I open it up a notch at a time. On some of my favourite reels I may open up fully and cast an easy free spool for maximum distance, but then I have to rely on my rod-casting thumb to brake the reel manually as the lure nears the water. In most lure fishing you can get away with the odd bird's nest on the reel, but with heavy jerkbaits, the mess may be just a bit difficult to unravel. Incidentally, if you do get a bad braid tangle don't get frustrated but try pulling loops gently, perhaps using a pin to ease 'knots' a little. Be patient. It is often worth it because an untangled braid rarely has the same memory as untangled monofil and the line, after a quick pull/stretch, will be perfectly usable. With monofil this can be far from certain.

So you have a multiplier in your hands for the first time – what do you do? Set up the reel on the rod, plus your chosen trace and lure. Now, if you want to ignore my advice of the last paragraph and wish to begin at optimum casting mode for that lure, then hold the tackle at 45 degrees to the horizontal and free the spool. If the lure travels quickly to the deck, it is too loose. Alter the setting a bit. When you need to jerk the rod tip upwards a little to set the lure sliding downwards, you have it about right. It isn't free-spool exactly, but it is close to the optimum casting setting for that lure. The centrifugal brake should save you any embarrassment.

You are now a fully fledged jerkbait angler, armed and ready to go. Don't get carried away with the 'force'! Use all the approach work and craft outlined earlier in this book – and get into training!

6 Rubber Jigs and Lures

Back in the 1970s, Ken Whitehead and I were using rubber eels and worms for piking. They didn't seem to me to be particularly productive and I eventually gave up on them. We featured quite a few in our early book on lure fishing (*Spinners, Spoons and Wobbled Baits*) because Ken did rather well with them, especially the long red wiggly worms. These had, usually, two singles stuck in them which, at the time, seemed inadequate to me. Ken, however, seemed to have no trouble: if the pike took he gave a pull rather than a strike and the hooks seemed to take purchase. I preferred my plugs.

My conversion occurred in the 1980s when someone sent me a box of rubber fish lookalikes with transverse tails. They cast like bullets, worked well, the hook rig was good – and they caught pike well. I'll recount an incident which hammered home

the point not just to me but to the gamekeeper on our lake. I recall the day well because it was dismal, grey and the rain fell steadily. I sat in warmth and comfort under my brolly with two deadbaits out in front of me. Not a run. I was doing what I do best in angling, namely being lazy. Then the gamekeeper, Hugh, came along for a chat and a coffee, squeezed under my brolly – and then he saw the heap of rubber fish on the ground. He laughed out loud, declaiming that anglers would buy anything and cast serious doubts on my statement that they caught pike well. I always have the lure rod with me even when bait fishing, so I put on a trout lookalike and, still sitting under the brolly, chucked it a good thirty yards out, let it sink to about a foot off the bottom then began a slow retrieve. It was taken by a fish of 8lb or so first cast. Hugh was tickled pink, so we then reeled in the deadbait rods

A rubber-tailed lure in firetiger, one of the most productive of all lure colours in predator fishing.

Basic lead-headed jigs. The tails are easily changed and often have to be.

Rubber frog, excellent amongst lily pads.

and I chucked out the rubber lures from my chair. I finished up with eight pike from about 5–9lb in thirty minutes or so. He was as convinced as I had been for quite some time that rubber lures, one day, would be revolutionary.

And now they are. The huge range of styles, colours and sizes, jigs and lookalikes means that you can do almost anything with them and catch almost anything. Fish in a water go off all lures in time, but rubber lures seem effective for just a bit longer – and the variety helps in this too, of course. Shortly after the day I mentioned above I obtained some rubber/plastic grubs with wiggly tails and lead heads. I fished them in sunken trees on the same lake and caught a number of good perch. I also had several fish – perch presumably – pull the rubber tail, stretch it, but avoid the hooks. This is a 'problem' with some jigs and rubber plugs. However, the experience doesn't seem to put the fish off and they often take a firmer grip the very next cast.

I've used these rubber lures for almost everything, most recently and spectacularly for Nile perch in Egypt's Lake Nasser. There they take other fish too, including

puffer fish, although these have a nasty habit of biting chunks out of the rubber body. When this happens you can conduct a little surgery, using an old lure, a razor blade or scissors, and some Araldite or superglue. Big fish will take small rubber lures, and 100lb+ Nile perch have fallen to lures only 3–4in long. It's probably the vibrating wobble that draws the fish, while the softness of the bait may make fish hang on just a little bit longer than they would on plastic or metal. You can dunk rubber lures in scents as well, although this ploy is certainly easier if you are casting from a boat, when you can avoid getting the goo all over your hands.

I'm not going to mention specific brands at this stage, although many are featured earlier in the book. The important thing is to get yourself a range of sizes, colours and types, plus spare lead heads and rubber bodies (and a tube of superglue). Rubber jigs and lures don't take up a deal of space in your bag so you can easily carry more when bank fishing than you'd otherwise do with traditional lures. Thus armed you can fish a great range of depths and swims from open to snag-ridden (many have single and

Bulldawg-style rubber lures can be fished shallow or deep, trolled or jerked.

On hitting the water, these lures continue to 'swim' away from the caster for a yard or so. Good for going under boats, bushes or logs.

protected hooks for snag fishing). And, of course, you can switch in a moment to fishing for zander, perch or pike, or whatever else. So far, I'm unaware of a predatory fish which won't fall for those lures, and that goes for sea fish and game fish. They are probably the most versatile group of lures available and even include one which, when it hits the water, continues to swim in the direction you have cast it, which is good for casting beneath overhanging bushes and tethered boats.

If there is a downside to rubber/plastic lures it is that some fish teeth can seriously damage their health, so a replacement or repair kit is always handy. Other plastic lures seem to have a coating which dissolves other lures quite quickly. I even had one recently which dissolved itself through the side of a plastic bucket. These types are fine in the water, but on the bank need wrapping in something resistant to their juices. Don't put them next to your camera or designer clothes.

7 Advanced Big-Water Trolling

By Gordon Burton

Many anglers have posed this question to me: what is my favourite method when pike fishing on the largest of our freshwaters? The answer I give is always the same, which is that whatever tactical approach I am catching pike on at any particular time is the most favourable. It is the same fishing with lures: What is my favourite? It is a pointless question really. How can I have one choice above all when there are hundreds of them in my lure boxes to suit so many different situations encountered while fishing. However, if I was forced to choose one method for all seasons when hunting the big pike and to a much lesser degree the ferox trout of the great lochs, then above all it would have to be trolling. No other method attracts my adventurous spirit more than this one. I love it. To me, it is an adventure every time I go afloat.

Many years ago I read of giant pike caught trolling from the vast waters of Ireland, Loughs Corrib, Ennel, Ree and Mask, and in particular John Garvin's one-time record of 53lb taken from Lough Conn. Way back then, most anglers trolled on the great waters by simply casting a lure astern of the boat and either motoring along or rowing. They were exceptionally good at it too and accounted for many great fish: giant pike and ferox trout, many salmon too. The late Fred Wagstaffe trolled on many big waters using varying tactics and was an inspiration in the early days of my trolling. Right from my earliest beginnings fishing on Scotland's Loch Ken in 1971 it

was my intention to really get to grips with using this method. Since those days, trolling has become a more varied method; in fact, it's become an art that takes a lot of skill to work all the different techniques.

In this chapter, it is my intention to put over the deadly effectiveness of trolling in

Gordon Burton with a 23½lb pike on 8in Depth Raider in 35ft of a Northern water. (Photograph courtesy of Gordon Burton)

A selection of trolling spoons. Note the homemade ones. Both Gordon and Barrie make their own. (Photograph courtesy of Gordon Burton)

deep-water situations and explain many of the techniques and different tactical approaches that I have used to take a huge number of big pike. Although pike are my number one target species I have accounted for lots of big perch taken on outsize lures, as well as a fair number of sea trout and a couple of fluke salmon, a few muskies and walleye and those leviathans of the deep, the ferox trout. Trolling is without doubt a fantastic method and one which permits the angler to exploit so many aspects of the varying habitats of these big-water predators. From the shallowest of flats to deep-lying humps, sunken valleys, troughs, deep-shelving cliff faces and deep weed lines, trolling will locate fish-holding spots by catching predators and will pull up the big ones too.

Trolling for me is a wonderful experience and I get a surge of adrenaline every single time I push my boat onto the water and it is a very rare session indeed that at least some of the fishing time is not spent trolling. It is not a back-up tactic for me when failing to get good results with other methods. Trolling demands the precision of steering the boat and controlling the lines, as well

as knowing more or less exactly where and how deep the lures are working at all times. It is very often my spearhead approach to catching fish and many are the times I have travelled to big waters to spend days just trolling. Many times have I read negative remarks about this super method but I will not go into detail here, other than to say that these critics have no trolling experience and don't know what they are talking about.

From flat-line trolling using both mono (I still use it) and braided lines, this method is simply trolling a lure on a long line without the aid of anything else, just the diving ability or weight of the lure to get down into the chosen depth contour. There are lots of floating-diving crankbaits that can dive very deep, below 30ft, using this technique. I can also troll lures well out abreast of the boat employing the use side planers. I have used a Wiley side planer and the Walleye planer board. The side planer is a floating rudder device that clips onto the main line. The lure is cast astern to the desired distance and then the line is slotted into the pressure clip and a securing attachment on the planer. Then lower the planer onto

Takes your breath away! A good pike on a lead-cored line. (Photograph courtesy of Gordon Burton)

the water and it will ride on its edge as it runs along the surface. The more line out, the further aside from the boat it will run. Using a planer board really is a great way to spread lures across a wide span astern of the boat, and if I so wished six rods could be used at the same time. When a fish slams its jaws on a lure and hooks itself, the line will rip free of the clip on the planer board, which will then slide down the line towards the fish. I use a 60lb test wire leader 3ft long with a large rubber bead over the knot at the connecting swivel and this acts as a stop to prevent the planer sliding all the way down

Taken on Red Hot Tiger pattern, Rapala Magnum. (Photograph courtesy of Gordon Burton)

the line and hitting the pike or predator fish in the head. Would you believe it, I have also seen film footage of a big muskie following and then actually striking a planer board.

Other methods I use to send my lures down to work in the deeps are employing the use of in-line leads, snap-on leads, lead-cored line and wire lines. The in-line leads I use are oval or half-moon shaped with a ring on each end that can be tied into the main line several feet ahead of the lure. I often use them up to 6oz in weight. They are not cumbersome to use and these weights will take lures very deep down. This is a very effective method to catch pike from deep water. I employed the use of this tactic when random trolling a 14cm Rapala Magum Countdown and a deep-diving 8in mirolure over a very deep area on Lake Stor-Treen in Sweden, taking big pike just off the bottom 15yd down. Snap-on leads are so easy to use and are simply a large pear-shaped bomb or Arlesey bomb connected to a special padded thumb pressure clip. Just like the in-line lead, I use one between 3–6oz as a rule, but sometimes a much heavier weight is used. A lead is easily

clipped up and will grip tight enough on the line so that it will not come off during the fighting antics of fish. If using a heavy lead bomb and it slips down a fine diameter braided line, I have changed line to 40lb test mono and a snap-lead seems to hold firm and not slip.

It was my privilege to be the first UK angler to test and review the Cannon easy-troll down-riggers for deep-water precision trolling, but in this chapter I am covering other tactics for fishing deep down. As with any method one must have full confidence in what they are doing. Whenever my lures are out 'pushing water' (at work trolling) and the rod tips are pulsating in unison with the lure action, I always have that 'any minute now' feeling of expectation that a rod will lash round in a deep bend and yet another big predator will have clamped its jaws onto a lure.

One big factor in the various fish-holding locations on huge bodies of water is the depth at which predators reside. In comparison to most of the waters we fish, the choice is far greater and big pike will often be caught from very deep water. At the

A selection of Gordon's trolling plugs, Depth Raiders, Grandmas, Cisco Kid, Jake and Black Magdawg. (Photograph courtesy of Gordon Burton)

Gordon's trolling crankbaits: Grandmas at the bottom, Depth Raiders at the top, and in-between are Mann's Stretch 25 and Hellcats Magnum, plus a Creek Chub Pikie. (Photograph courtesy of Gordon Burton)

very beginning of the 1970s and my first trolling sessions on Loch Ken, pike were caught deeper on lures than ever before, for example 30ft down trolling spoons on lead-cored line and what we now term an in-line lead. Over many years now I have taken big pike from dozens of the largest waters of England, Scotland, Ireland, Sweden and Canada below 30ft down to as deep 55ft when using precision deep-water trolling tactics, and no doubt much deeper when random zigzag trolling over much deeper water. It is surprising just how many big fish I see on the screen of my sonar unit suspended high up over very deep water – catching the wandering 'super-tankers', you might say. Lakes Windermere, Coniston, Derwent Water, Bassenthwaite; Lochs Lomond, Awe, Oich and Woodhall; and Loughs Kilglass, Key, Cloonfree, Bally-quirke, Skee and Muchno are amongst the many places that deep trolling has paid off.

Now let's deal with how best to go about tackling these big waters. When searching out large areas of open deep water I may use up to four rods at the same time, some-times more.

A longer rod of around 10ft is used in the outrigger rod rest directly outwards on each of the gunwales of the boat, while a shorter 6½ to 7ft medium-weight jerkbait-type rod is used at a shallow angle in rod rests off the stern of the boat. These rods are used in conjunction with ABU 5000 and 6000 series multiplier reels and also Shimano Moocher Plus 4000GT centre-pin reels, which are my top choice for trolling. All reels must have an audible drag system so that when a fish strikes a lure it will screech as line is torn from the reel. I cannot keep my eyes on up to four rod tips at the same time, so this is best way to keep in contact with the working rods at all times. The multipliers are loaded with braided lines of 30lb, 50lb and 65lb test which are used for all flat-line, in-line lead and side-planer trolling methods. Fireline is the most abrasion-resistant of all the braided lines I have used and it does withstand rough contact with rugged ground when trolling, whereas some other brands of braid have sheared off quite alarmingly.

The centre-pin reel is loaded with Cortland 27lb-test lead-cored line which is a

A planer board, less garish than the one Barrie uses. (Photograph courtesy of Gordon Burton)

Lure retrieval system used all over the world and essential for the boat angler. (Photograph courtesy of Gordon Burton)

different colour every 10yd, thereby more or less telling you exactly how much line is out behind the boat when fishing. A 10ft braided leader line is spliced on the end of the lead-core line, then a wire trace is tied to the end. This is an ideal line for taking lures like spoons and spinnerbaits deep down to 30ft on a shorter line length of 30–40yd, with no need for any added weight. Some people can be critical of it but I also use 30lb-test seven-strand wire line for some trolling. That is what it was designed for, trolling. The Moocher reel really is an efficient tool for fishing lead-cored line and it is also used for fishing with the wire line, but any good-quality large drum reel will do the job. This wire will cut lures deep down on a short line, just the job for working deep-diving crank-bait lures tight up to deep outcrops where fish may be holding close up. It is ideal for working in very rocky locations such as are found on some big waters, Ireland's Lough Mask being the prime example. I recall deep trolling in extremely rocky areas along the eastern shore and islands on Mask; it was positively frightening. Pinnacles of jagged rock reached up from the bottom and running a line against such an object sheared through it like cutting butter. I lost

a few lures on those deep-water hazards and for that reason I got into using seven-strand wire lines to combat such situations. Hard chrome rings are essential on a rod, otherwise extensive trolling with wire line will groove inferior rings, resulting in badly kinked line. Initially, it was something of a surprise to feel the solid thump of a big-taking fish on this kind of line, due to its non-stretchiness and weight.

Length of Trolling Lines

This is something I have greatly experimented with and in order to put my lures where I require them to run, and not spook fish, a line of 50yd length is ideal when flat-lining. On occasions I may go to a longer or shorter line depending upon a sudden change of lure and situation. On calm, very clear water, I may extend to a line as long as 80yd. I call this my 'tail-gunner' rod, running a lure way behind the other baits and it is often surprising how many fish this rod catches. In general in very clear water I prefer to have lures trolled on a longer line, as it may give fish time to settle after a boat has just passed over them. Even when flat-lining, with the lines and length I advise, it

Four rods on the troll. The centre pin rod holds the lead-cored line. (Photograph courtesy of Gordon Burton)

is possible to get some big floating-diving crankbaits, such as Big Ernie, Hooker and Cisco Kid, below 35ft. If trolling in rough wave conditions I use lead-core or wire lines, as these will take the lures down to 35ft on shorter lines. To measure line distance one can use a reel with a line-counter facility, tie a stop-knot on the line at the required length, or use an indelible marking pen to put the distance marks on lighter-coloured braided lines.

My sonar unit is a Bottom Line Tournament Champion which has many useful facilities, including temperature probe and speedometer. There is never any guesswork as to the speed at which I am trolling. It is a fantastic piece of equipment for the big-water fisherman. A sonar unit is an absolute necessity for the trolling angler because it cannot be done effectively without such equipment.

The Best Speeds at Which to Pull Lures Along

I always know the speeds at which my lures are working and those between 1–5mph are the ones I use in order to get my lures to a required depth. These speeds do trigger strikes and catch big fish. When suddenly surging the boat forwards at an increased speed I have experienced some tremendous rod-wrenching strikes that put a frightening bend in the rod. I firmly believe, too, that many of the big fish I catch on the troll are already on the move, hunting along depth contours or cruising through deep open water and are primed and ready to strike the lures, even those lures running at increased speeds.

When fishing multi-rods and working different lures at various depths, a lot of water is thoroughly searched and fish are caught at whatever levels they are hunting. When the lures are down in action a close eye must be kept on the rod tips to ensure they judder and pulsate in unison with the throbbing action of the lure. A still rod tip means a lure is not working right and probably will not catch fish. When fishing in this manner it is not uncommon to get multiple hook-ups, with two takes coming at once; on a couple of occasions I have even had three fish hooked at the same time. The first time this happened was on Loch Ken nearly 30

A homemade downrigger system. Good commercially made ones are now readily available, as are boat rod rests.

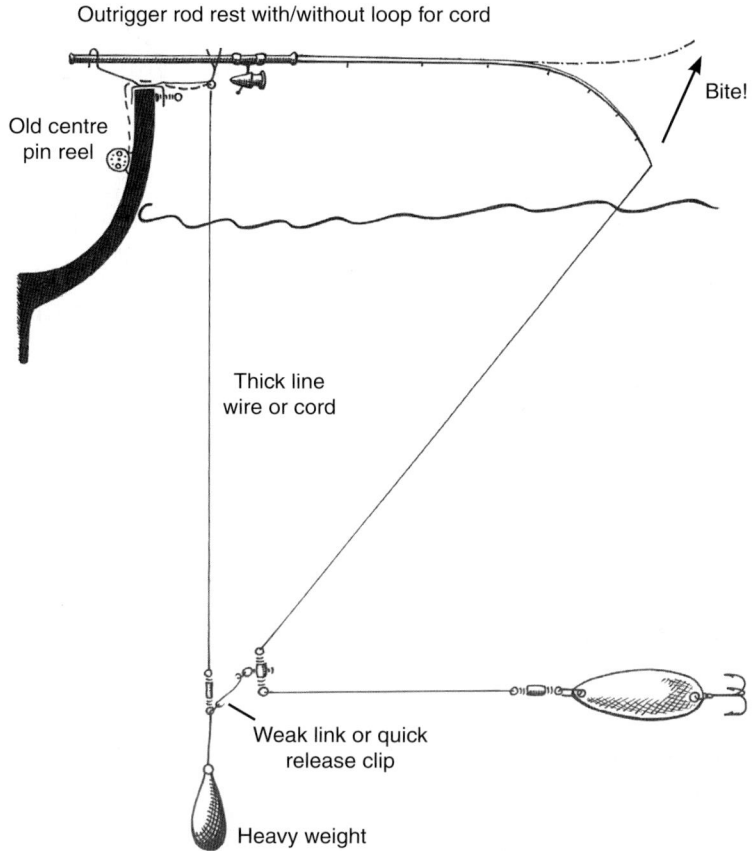

Outrigger rod rest with/without loop for cord

Bite!

Old centre pin reel

Thick line wire or cord

Weak link or quick release clip

Heavy weight

years ago. We had just got the lures down when the first strike came, followed almost immediately by two more takes. This being in the very early days of my trolling, it was sensational for something like this to take place, but it has only happened once since, although double hook-ups are not rare. With trolling, you have to expect the unexpected; for example, I know of a 20lb pike that took two lures at the same time, grabbing one while smashing into the other with a swish of its tail. It is fun and games controlling all the lines when such events take place. If you are trolling alone, get the other lines upwind of the boat, which will then drift away from them and not cause any tangles. I have done this many times

when trolling alone, although if trolling in a fair wind and big waves then I will usually work with just two rods.

Boat control and steering is of utmost importance if trolling with several rods at the same time. A cross over of lines or a crankbait or spoon making contact with another line will cause the lures to rotate, resulting in a terrible line-twisting tangle, so be warned when making a wide, sweeping turnaround.

Without any doubt, lipped diving crankbaits are the most versatile of all lures for trolling and I use them more than any other lure. I have now taken 20lb+ pike on thirty-one different crankbaits and these are some of my best deep-water fish catchers: Rapala

Magnum, Cisco Kid, Ernie, Invincible, Hooker, Creek Chub Pikie, Giant Grandma, Plough, Big N, Bomber LA, Triple D, Believer and the Joe Bucher Depth Raider range. Depth Raiders are fantastic crankbaits for deep-water fishing and I have taken 20lb+ plus pike on seven different models. I reckon to own one or two crankbaits that have now pushed a thousand miles of water on the troll. All of these lures are top-class fish catchers in depth ranges of between 20–50ft down when flat-lining. I also fix a split-ring on the connecting eye on every one of the lures, as this makes for a better lure action. Use only the strongest of rings because trolling tests tackle to the limit and you don't want to tell of a lost giant because of faulty tackle. Don't forget to ensure that all hooks are kept sharp.

Spoons have brought me the greatest numbers of fish in a session, sometimes topping thirty pike in a day. Kuusamo Professor, Atlantic Spoon, Gator-Back, Wabler, Flasher, Red-Eye Wriggler and a whole host of homemade copper, brass and stainless steel spoons have produced big pike for me. Some of the lightweight spoons are perfect for trolling in very shallow water. A ball-bearing swivel is used on the wire leader when trolling spoons to prevent line twist if a lure goes into a spin instead of wobbling. In-line and snap-on leads are great for getting these lures deep down. The leads I use vary from 2oz to over 1lb. They are indeed very effective pieces of equipment. Cast a lure out to a set distance, say 20yd, and then clip on a 2–4oz lead and let the same length of line out and this will take the spoon deep down. When using the heaviest lead it will suspend on the line almost directly down below the rod tip, almost like using a mini down-rigger. Lightweight spoons and even shallow running crankbaits can be pulled very deep down on this tackle. When a fish is hooked it's played in until the lead can be reached and unclipped, so easy. A friend of mine

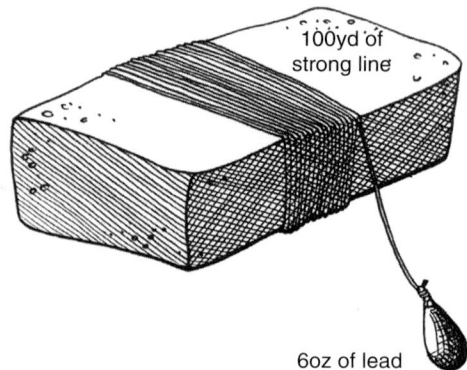

A neat way of relocating a taking zone, thrown over the side of the boat at the time of the strike. The block can be polystyrene or a plastic bottle. The GPS is sometimes slower!

recently caught two 27lb pike which took a crankbait fished 45ft down (with the aid of a snap-lead to take the lure so deep). Only recently, I was trolling over water between 40–60ft deep and spotted a number of big arches just off the bottom and my mate said, 'Let's get the heavy [4–6oz snap-ons] leads on and scratch their backs.' We did, and we caught 'em.

Heavy 2–3oz spinnerbaits, such as the Grinder, Brute and Bionic Bucktail, also do the job and can be fished in the above manner, or as I did the first time I trolled such a lure 30ft deep: on wire line. This resulted in several big pike of 20lb+ from Ireland's Lough Muchno. At present, although I have caught lots of big fish trolling soft plastics at shallow depths, they are rarely used for deep-water trolling.

Sizes of Lures for Trolling

A great deal of my trolling time is spent hunting big fish and so I tend to use the larger sized lures, those in the range 8–12in, because these consistently catch me more big fish. However, this is not to say I don't use the smaller sizes; in fact, just recently I have taken fish from 20lb to almost 25lb on two patterns of Baby Depth Raider, perch pattern and firetiger. Super Shad Rap, Windcheater, Monster Shad and Lil Ernie are smaller lures that have pulled big fish from the deeps. I will also troll some rolling action jerkbaits deep down and one of Loz Harrop's Darter range caught a 14lb+ ferox for me. This big trout struck as it smacked off a rock hump 35ft down, fished on 80yd of lead-cord line when trolling in the Pass O' Brander stretch on Scotland's Loch Awe.

Lure Colours

Regarding the best lure colours and patterns, there are so many to choose from it can be demoralizing for a newcomer, but follow natural patterns like silver shad, perch, pike, gold shiner for very clear water conditions, even when fishing deep down, and use all sorts of gaudy bright choices for darker deep-water trolling. Thirty years ago on Loch Lomond a friend and I discovered that flo-orange was a good colour trolled deep down and since then this colour, along with all sorts of flo-colour patterns, have caught big pike, perch and ferox. I well remember deep trolling for ferox on Loch Arkaig and hooking nine fish, with every lure used having a distinct blend of flo-orange in the pattern. Firetiger is a truly great fish-catching pattern that has landed me many big pike and two big ferox. Flo-orange belly perch pattern is another super fish-catching pattern for big pike and ferox. In fact, as far as I am aware the largest trout ever caught on a lure in the Lake District came to a lady, Leslie Robbins, whom I was guiding on Windermere, and that fish of 15lb 4oz took a flo-perch Depth Raider when trolling tight to a deep sheering drop-off 30ft down. Red Hot Tiger is a top catcher and gave me a twenty-seven-pounder when trolling on a bleak, freezing winter's day. I am in no doubt that these big predators can see the lures deep down and hit them hard. Joe Bucher even produced two of my top deep-water finishes: Depth Raiders in

And action! This time using wire line on Loch Ken. Note that Gordon is bending into the fish, not tickling it. (Photograph courtesy of Gordon Burton)

master-blaster and psycho-perch patterns, both top-notch colours.

The knowledge of the lure's running depth is crucial at all times. When first starting out, much trial and error is required in order to find out how deep a lure will dive to, although many lures will now come with depth recommendations on the boxes. How to learn? When the lures are out and working at the best speeds simply guide the boat gradually up shallower until a certain lure bumps the bottom. Then take a note of the depth and pace of boat and very soon a whole variety of lures are catalogued as to what depths they will dive to. It is interesting to note just how many different lures enter the same grouping. Once the system is worked out, it becomes easy to steer the lures over rising humps on the bottom by simply slowing the boat down, which will cause floating crankbaits to rise and run higher in the water.

Large deep-diving countdown crankbaits will run very deep at a slower pace, say 2mph, and these are what to use when searching the 40–50ft depth bands. I once read an article on trolling in which the writer advised tripping the bottom with lures to provoke strikes, but I would like to know just where this tactic would work successfully. Most of the waters I have fished have rocky bottom structures and when a lipped crankbait collides with solid rock the result is usually the lip being smashed off. It is vital that the lures are running free of the bottom at all times or the hooks will pick up debris. This will deaden the action of the lures and predatory fish will not take them if the hooks are clogged with weed and leaves. There is one water I fished where I used a bottom-bumping tactic. Lake of the Woods in Canada is a place with vast areas of flat, bald rock reefs and bottom and grinding a lure across this flat structure produces big fish. I know this for sure, because a

45in muskie pulverized my Depth Raider at such a location.

Depth-chart maps are a great guideline. Unless I have a depth-chart map of any new water, my first aim is to motor far and wide using my Bottom Line sonar equipment, scanning the offshore drop-offs and deeps in order to pinpoint attractive-looking features that in turn may have big fish in residence. All likely trolling routes are marked off on the map as new areas are looked over. Use marker buoys to pinpoint deep-lying features as this assists in making close trolling passes, which can sometimes be crucial in catching fish. The depths usually range from 20ft to below 50ft or more, with the 30ft level often being a red-hot depth band that produces many big fish. Once this task has been done and a good-looking area planned out, I take the boat well out from the area, get all the lures out and working at the chosen depths, then sweep the boat back over the planned-out stretch of water following the chosen contour as closely as possible. Be constantly aware of the depth on the sonar, so that any sudden changes can be taken into account and the lures kept running free of the bottom.

The troller must constantly vary the pace and movement of the boat and zigzag or roll the boat from side to side in order to change the action of the lures, as such actions provoke strikes. Trolling the contours of deep-lying humps, ridges, troughs and walls as deep down as 50ft is all about precision. Working lures around such features is a bit difficult to begin with, but by steering the boat up and across a ridge then turning the boat back along the deep edge it will keep the lures running at the same depth and close to the original contour. This is the way to catch big fish tight to such features. The entire location will need to be motored over back and forth repeatedly for a lengthy period to ensure it has been well searched out before moving on.

Look out for pods or even big clouds of prey fish showing up on the sonar screen. In many instances you can bet big pike will be close by. In the case of char shoals, when locating these fish very deep down, even as much as 100ft, it is not uncommon to see a few large predators in very close proximity. So when these tight shoals of fish are pinpointed it can really pay off to work all around them. During one short morning spell a friend and I boated seventeen pike, including three double hook-ups trolling over such an area. Any spot that produces a fish is marked off on the map for future reference. I have pulled three big fish from the same tiny trough in the bottom, so it pays to take note of such features for future reference. On some of the large waters I fish, where there are large areas of water of depths between 30–50ft, I put out a multi-rod system and simply random-troll all over the place, catching wandering fish.

Dealing with the Strike

I have gone over working the lures, so now let us look at the strike when a big fish slams its jaws on a lure deep down in the water. The set of the drag on the reel is absolutely crucial, so make certain the drag is set accordingly – it needs to yield to a taking fish yet be tight enough to hook it securely. In most instances, when the fish strikes the lure the rod lashes round in a deep bend and it seems like the lure has snagged. If it's a big fish it will feel like you have hooked a dead weight, a bag of sand with fins. The fish hook themselves because the forward momentum of the boat pulls the hooks home. Then comes that tell-tale solid jag and thud on the end of the line which tells you that you have hooked a hawg. A tight drag-set is needed to prevent the line slipping when trolling a big-lipped deep-diving crankbait against water pressure. Too tight a drag can result in a crack-off or the hooks being torn from the fish's mouth when it strikes the lure. I have even seen rods wrenched round and smashed.

Now let me take you back to the first pike I ever caught when trolling on Loch Ken in the beginning of 1970s. A tremendous strike came to an Efgeeco Piker spoon with two large Jardine leads, fixed just above the trace to help get the lure deep and trolled 80yd astern of the boat. My first ever fish was hooked on the troll and my immediate thoughts were that I had hooked a monster when I felt the weight on the end of the line, but then the fish jumped, revealing itself to be just around double figures. All that

On Last Mountain Lake, Saskatchewan, Canada.
(Photograph courtesy of Gordon Burton)

Barrie trolling on Lough Mask in Ireland, using a telescopic but powerful rod. Shortly after this was taken, so was a 20lb pike!

water pressure against the fish had kidded me otherwise, but it was an exciting start to my fishing adventures just the same.

Fishing on any of the biggest waters means that the angler must expect to encounter inclement weather conditions at any time, varying from calm to wild and windy, in a very short space of time. I've experienced such events many times, including fish hooked in wild weather conditions. Now I regularly troll in ominous conditions; it is a wild day indeed that drives me off the water. It pays to know the capability any boat you fish from and always wear a life jacket. Even in the freezing conditions of winter, I will still troll – I've caught plenty of big pike when the high ground surrounding the lakes has been covered in snow.

When trolling with a partner, when a big fish is hooked, there should be no problem; while one plays the fish, the other takes care of handling the other lines and controls the boat. Now let us assume I am alone trolling an eastern shoreline on a big loch, with a strong westerly wind putting a good wave on the water and a big pike strikes the lure. The outboard engine is immediately switched out of gear, the wrenching rod is quickly taken from the rod rest and I pull into the fish. This is when prior preparation can be vital. To prevent the boat being swept into the rocky shoreline, a suitable mud-weight or lightweight plough anchor with a good length of rope to spare is kept close at hand in the boat. Secure the rope and have it in position over whatever cleat or runner is fixed on the front of the boat, so that when a fish is hooked this anchor can be easily dropped overboard. The boat will then swing round, bows into the wind. I once hooked a twenty-seven-pounder trolling in a gale, and I could barely stand up in the rocking boat, but when the anchor went down it stabilized and prevented the boat being swept ashore. I hauled aboard a big fat hawg of a fish. This may sound a bit dodgy, but that is part and parcel of trolling on these wonderful waters.

8 Lightweight Lure Fishing

Many years ago Ken Whitehead (i.e. Deryck Swift) and I met up as keen lure fishermen and found we were both into lightweight lure fishing. In my case it was because I fished a lot of very small waters, ponds and rivers, where the fish ran up to 3lb or so. I couldn't see the point of heavy pike gear so went down to 6lb line, a small rod, very fine trace and small lures. I caught pike, perch, chub, brown, sea and rainbow trout primarily. Occasionally I had a big pike. One tiny Cambridge stream produced one well over 10lb – the steam was only twice as wide as the length of the fish. Ken was using light tackle because he preferred it and in this sense was closer to the present day outlook of the fine tackle experts such as Peter Crowther. We included a bit on light tackle work in our first book (*Spinners, Spoons and Wobbled Baits*) and, it must be said, we had slight philosophical differences on the matter. For me, it is wrong to fish too light if big fish are expected or being pursued actively. For Ken this was quite sporting. I think today's specialists have it better argued than either Ken or I. They aim, by their delicate techniques, to induce a greater variety of fish species to take lures, roach, tench, bream, ruffe, and so on. If they are seeking big pike, they'll use big pike gear.

To get back to Ken and I … he wasn't impressed by my small telescopic (made in Taiwan and still going strong, incidentally) and showed me his cut-down fly rod. Ken's opinion was that the main purpose of fly rods was to have their butts hacked

A selection of Barrie's lures for lightweight lure fishing. They fit into a small maggot tin.

Playing a wild rainbow trout in New South Wales, taken on a tiny Mepps spinner.

off to make lightweight spinning rods. He made one for me, as a gift, and I have it to this day. It's a little soft in its action, but as one is using only 4–5lb bs line this doesn't matter, as the lures are consistently small and the hooks likewise. In fact, a lot of Ken's lightweight lure fishing has been carried out with single hooks.

Most species of fish are predatory at some stage of their life cycle or at some time of the year, and many are cannibals, eating their own fry once the fry reach an inch or two. Lightweight lure fishing aims to exploit this tendency by presenting tiny lures in front of a likely fish or shoal of fish. It's a bit like nymph fishing for trout I suppose; certainly

Big chub, small lure. (Photograph courtesy of Eric Wright)

the casting and retrieving is all done in a relatively slow and delicate fashion compared to most lure fishing. Richard Walker trotted the steam with his flies and nymphs beneath a float, to catch dace, roach and chub (I've tried this and it works, my best roach going 1lb 12oz) and you could use this technique with tiny lures too. An alternative is to use those line indicators which many fly fishermen use – a kind of small float, brightly coloured, which indicates a take. Or, if your preferred line is a floating braid, you could attach a tiny indicator at the junction of (floating) braid and (sinking) fluorocarbon trace.

As you can see, everything becomes very delicate and very touchy-feely when compared with most other lure fishing. And it grades into fly fishing doesn't it? You'll still catch perch and pike and chub, but other surprises too. I plan to try this approach on a water I have recently discovered where the tench are predatory (*see* Chapter 9). I'd strongly advise you to give it a go. Talk about travelling light. And even a perch of 12oz feels like a real achievement, which it is.

By now you will have realized that I like philosophical twists and there is one to do with lightweight lure fishing. I'm not referring to the chance of hooking something too powerful for the tackle – we all cope with that in our own way – no, I'm referring to what happens if you follow lightweight lure fishing to its logical conclusion. Does using a plastic maggot, worm, fly or even sweetcorn qualify as lure fishing? It's not that far removed, is it, from casting a 1in-long plug intended for rudd or roach? Perhaps the distinction is on how you propel it. For example, it's fly fishing if you use a fly rod and bait fishing if you use a float or ledger. I

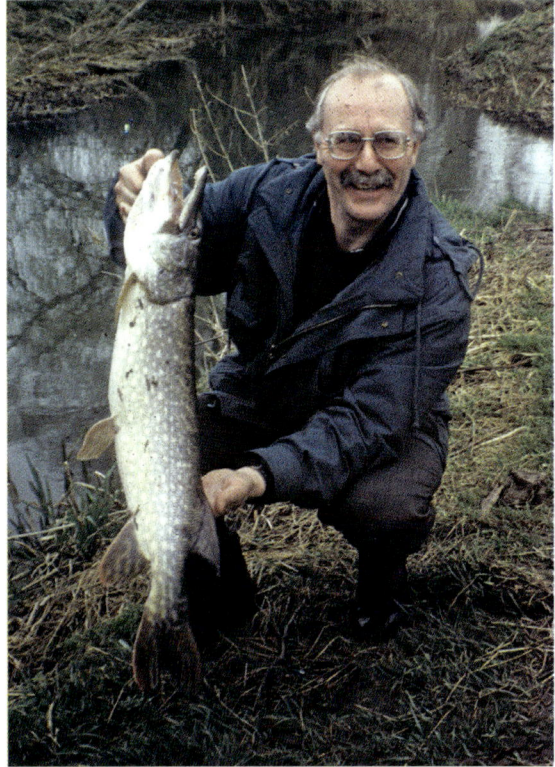

Nice pike from a tiny river in Cambridgeshire.

recently caught some nice rudd on a plastic maggot and on a plastic sweetcorn, simply by dapping them below the rod tip (as I used to do with plastic houseflies for chub, many years ago). On the same day I roll-casted a fly line baited with a plastic maggot and also with a plastic sweetcorn grain, and also caught rudd, roach and one bream. But I couldn't cast these 'lures' without a casting weight. What about an Olivetti on the line? The conclusion to be drawn from the above is how very lightweight lure fishing grades down into ordinary bottom fishing, and vice versa.

9 Chub, Perch and Other Coarse Fish Species

It follows from Chapter 8 that if you adopt such approaches you are likely to catch almost anything that swims, but chub and perch are more traditionally associated with spinning, and indeed, turn up occasionally on ordinary pike spinning tackle. When I looked back to my diaries for the 1950s and early 1960s, they were packed with catches of perch on spinners, almost all on small mackerel spinners or the small sizes of Colorados, plus a few on the now extinct Plucky Bait plug (a rubber plug). Small pike featured prominently too, so I soon realized that wire traces were necessary. Most wire traces were very dark-coloured and heavy and I did feel detracted from the perch results, so I simply put a couple of link swivels in front of the spinner, especially in swims where most of the fish caught were perch.

Perch far outnumbered pike anyway and sizes ranged from about ½lb to nearly 2lb, fish nearer the latter being more common. Later on, I've had them over 3lb, but never a 4lb fish. Dick Walker always reckoned that a piece of feather on the tail treble of perch spinners – something like roach tail, so a Rhode Island Red feather – was an advantage. Certainly when a perch strikes it quite commonly attacks the tail of the lure and usually just grabs the tail treble. I did try Rhode Island Red chicken feathers, but found a turn or two of red wool just as effective. I think the perch are attracted in this way, but care should be taken that additives do not destroy the action of the lure: they do if you add too much. For some unearthly reason on only two occasions I have added a worm to the tail treble. It worked both times, but I suppose when I go lure fishing I don't think to put a bag of worms on board.

Barrie with chub on artificial crayfish, caught on Yorkshire's River Ure.

*A good bream on a 6in Jim Vincent spoon, Lough
Garnafailagh, Athlone, Ireland.*

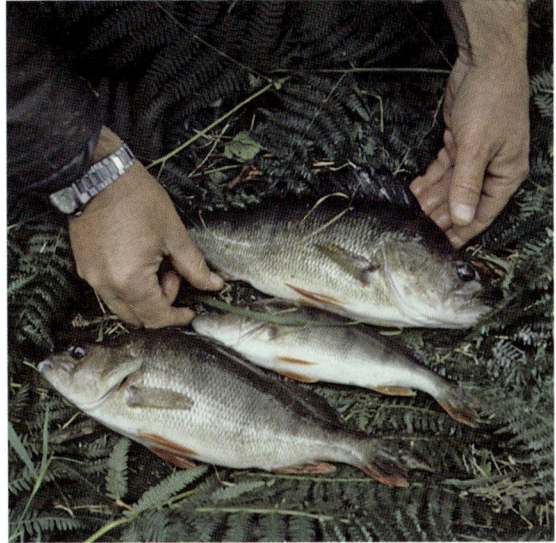

A nice bag of perch to spinnerbait.

Almost all lures work for perch. I have had
quite a few on spinnerbaits, for example.
And large plugs often catch small perch. On
one water where I was catching many fish
over 1lb, often on successive casts, I tried
both retaining and returning the fish immediately, just to see if it had any effect on the
strike rate. My feeling was that returned
fish did swim back to the shoal and put
them off. So I began returning perch quite
some distance away from where they were
caught. Another thing I noticed from personal experience was that although I did
quite well on lures, the bigger fish tended
to fall to worm or bait in the same swims.
Whether this is generally true I don't know,
but perch are cagey fish, of that there is no
doubt. I know two waters with good perch
where they simply will not look at a lure.
Not mine anyway.

Because of the revolution in pike trace
materials it is now possible to fish for perch
with confidence using traces that are, if
anything, less conspicuous than the line.
Line, too, is superb these days and a 10lb

braid is almost too thin. Monofil of 6lb bs
is also sufficient. You always have the line
twist problem with bar spoons and I don't
like adding an anti-kink lead up-trace. It
may not make a jot of difference and others
don't seem too worried, but I think it is why
I tend to use tiny plugs and spoons, rather
than spinners. I have had some lovely perch
between 2lb and just over 3lb using very
small plugs and little jigs too; it really is a
delightful way to fish.

The chub is another species which falls
readily to lures but, again, I wonder if the
biggest ones do. I have had a few 4lb fish
on lure, but never a 5lb fish. The approach
work of the angler to chub swims has to
be even more cautious than when perch
fishing and, if you drop off a chub, move
swim immediately. Spoons, primarily, and
plugs have taken most of my chub, rather
than spinners and it may be that spinners
are just too unnatural. But I'm not what I'd
call a successful chub angler and it may be
that others do rate spinners. I know that
the modern rubber jigs do work well and,

Jeremy Wade on the Amazon with a Peacock Bass, to crankbait.

Big red-bellied piranhas, all to crankbaits on the Amazon. They looked even better in the pan.

as with the perch family fish, I'm always happier using a colour which resembles somewhat the prey of the chub. I once had a nice 4lb fish on artificial crayfish fished sink and draw whilst I was on the River Ure with Bill Winship. There are several crayfish-like lures which do work well with chub.

Chub fight in a unique way in my experience. They go directly at any snag in the swim. Perch will transfer a hook to a reed stem with great skill, but a chub almost mugs the snag. I remember getting a Yorkshire 4lb fish from a tiny still water. There was only one snag in the water, a patch of bulrushes about a yard across. The chub hit it so hard the whole growth shook. Fortunately, the chub had taken a small

Norwich spoon about 1½in long and was well hooked on its only treble. Small spoons do produce plenty of chub. They do not seem to fall for giant plugs, at least not in my experience, and they differ from perch in this respect at least. Another lure which works well for chub is anything approaching a fly in appearance and size, adorned with hair and feather; they take flies readily enough, of course, but they also take those nearly flies used by sea trout anglers.

Bream take lures fairly often. I think my own catches have been in March and June in the UK and in May in Ireland. This suggests that their predatory tendencies are seasonal, possibly linked to aggression at the time of the spawning period, or to fry feeding at the same time, possibly also

Arawana of 8lb, from a lake in the flooded forest of the Amazon.

A deceived chub. (Photograph courtesy of Eric Weight)

Crayfish. These do deceive chub. Good for pike too.

A chub to a bar spoon with rubber worm additions. (Photograph courtesy of Eric Weight)

cannibalism. One catch I had in June from a Fenland drain was of five fish all over 5lb. On the Great Ouse at Ten Mile Bank I had a 6lb+ fish in March and another catch of big fish in March from a different Fenland drain. And in Ireland in May I've had several over the years, mostly over 7lb each and mostly while I have been pike trolling. All these fish, without exception, fell to an elongate Jim Vincent style spoon about 6in long. I haven't caught a bream on any other lure at all, despite showing them lures a million times. So if you want to try big bream on lures I'd suggest March and June, unless you fish in the Close Season. Use a spoon, but, most importantly, find a big shoal of bream.

Tench can be predatory and certainly cannibalistic. I know one water where every time I use a little rubber jig in summer, quite large tench attack it – but they pull the rubber tail and then let go. I've yet to catch one like this. But I did get a fish over 6lb from the same water, in winter, and it took a fairly large plug (a crankbait in perch colours). This was no accident; it hit the lure hard just as I was about to lift it from the water, so it was seriously in pursuit. What is more, I saw it hit the lure so I knew from the start that I was playing a tench. Whether tench can be induced to fall for lures regularly I'm not sure. Perhaps when more anglers are using the techniques mentioned in Chapter 8 we might find out.

Carp, of course, are better known to have predatory or scavenging instincts and they fall to small deadbaits fairly often, especially on some waters. But they take lures too. My own experience is limited, but I recall my son getting a nice one from a Cambridgeshire gravel pit – it took a bar spoon (Veltic) cleanly in the mouth. Similarly, I was fishing on a Northampton pit with Jim Baxter, the editor of the *Sheffield Angling Telegraph*, when he had a double figure common, also on a bar spoon (a Mepps, if I recall correctly). Both these fish gave wonderful scraps. Jeremy was spinning for perch at the time and had only light tackle. Carp have fairly often been

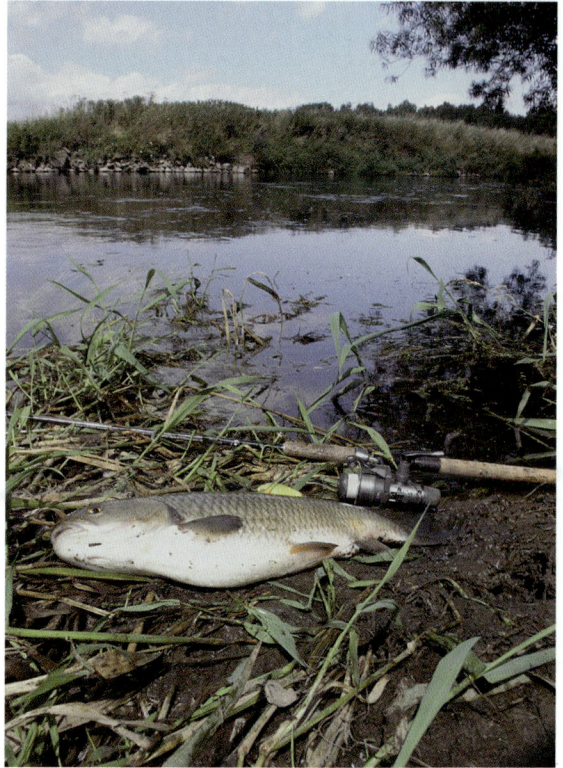

A chub on crankbait. (Photograph courtesy of Eric Weight)

reported on lures, but whether anything could be made of this I'm not sure. And as for eels, which have occasionally taken lures (*see* Chapter 15), I don't think we should hold our breath.

10 Zander

Spinning for zander got off to a slow and inauspicious start in England. In the 1960s plenty of zander fell to baits but the idea grew up that they didn't take lures regularly, despite evidence to the contrary from Europe and from walleye fishers in North America. Of course, as a rule all lure fishing is a little slower in the winter months and so most zander anglers fish for them with baits. Nevertheless, I caught lots of zander on lures through the late 1960s, 1970s and 1980s and it was only towards the end of that period, the 1990s specifically, that others began to get involved – I'd written about it often enough so it is rather puzzling that it didn't catch on sooner. Because of the way things developed it would probably be instructive if I gave my account more or less in the way I made my discoveries.

The first fish were by accident, naturally, and put down as flukes. One even fell to a paternoster lead which it grabbed as I retrieved the gear up a break of slope. Not long after, I had one chase an Arlesey bomb up a similar slope … so I offered them small bar spoons. It didn't work too well, though a few tiny zander of 8oz–1lb showed an interest. It was only when I began to use fish-like, elongated spoons that I began to get results. I began with standard-sized Tobys, then smaller versions, but the simple, egg-shaped, Norwich spoon in *silver* began to get results that were better. I used spoons up to around 2in long at the most. Some were painted red on the concave surface,

silver metal on the convex, but plain silver worked best. These were not small zander by the way, unless you count 4–7lb fish as small. Another spoon which produced results had a fish pattern painted on one side – a perch, a roach, and so on (Renosky lures). I began to think that spoons which roughly resembled prey fish worked better and I still think that is an important factor. Pike go for any manner of bizarre lure, but zander are more selective – like perch family species in general.

After this early phase with spoons I turned to plugs. Once again, the prey-fish lookalikes worked best and little fat silver plugs like the Middy S worked well. I did not use big plugs at this stage, even though I'd had big zander on big baits.

The catch rates were interesting too. As long as I was in a zander water with a fair head of fish I was taking up to eight fish in a session, which was usually from just before dawn into a few hours of daylight. Or I'd fish the other way round, the last couple of hours into the dark. Morning was better in my experience. Next came night spinning. This also produced fish, but still not quite as well as the pre-dawn and dawn periods. In the dark I also caught on surface plugs and my best lure-caught zander to date, of 9½lb, fell to a jointed Creek Chub fished on the surface. I haven't caught zander on surface lures during the day. As an aside perhaps, I ought to mention that I have had quite a few double-figure zander on baits but not on lures. I think this is probably because I haven't lure-fished much on my zander bait waters.

Probably the next important discovery was that zander fell to spinnerbaits. I was surprised at this, given the lack of success with bar spoons and the fact that spinner-baits do not much resemble prey fish. I've done best on the Relief Channel, Cut-Off Channel and Lower Great Ouse, all in the Cambridgeshire Fens. Two kinds of takes proved commonest: one, out in open water, deep, near the bottom; and two, as the lure came up the slope. In the first case, I worked the spinnerbait *on* the bottom so that it was kicking up 'dust' clouds. This only works conveniently if the bottom is reasonably clean that season. Most of the takes were of a gentle dragging nature – similar to a foul-up on the weed – rather than a full-blooded thump. Every 'drag' had to be treated as a bite. The takes up-slope were much more savage, with the zander often rocketing up the slope at high speed, hitting the lure at the last possible moment, then diving back down the slope, whipping round the rod end. These did surprise me a lot, given the zander's rather lackadaisical battle strategy once hooked. Certainly they are much faster fish than you might think.

Next came rubber baits and jigs. Ken Whitehead and I were into these in the 1970s, for pike, but now the jigs, usually Rapala hard jigs, began to take zander. Early rubber baits in the UK were fine for pike (for example, rubber eels and rubber sand eels), but they only came into their own for zander when the modern rubber jigs arrived. But all jigs work for zander, some very well indeed. I soon discovered that you didn't need to fish off bridges or boats. They work just as well from the bank

providing you choose the right weight, size and action for the water in question and, in particular for its slope up to your feet. For example, you wouldn't use the same jigs in the relatively deep River Delph as you would in the nearby shallower Old Bedford River – at least, I wouldn't.

It could be my overactive imagination, but I still feel that even with modern jigs it pays to use colours that the zander might select because they are not too unlike the prey species – in colour, if nothing else. So far I haven't mentioned water colour. It is common knowledge that zander feed well in pea-soupers. And they do so too on lures. You just have to be brave and forget all about pike. For me, in very coloured water, spinnerbaits and modern rubber jigs have worked well. I'm less confident with the other lures I have mentioned.

Lastly, I'll mention the big lures. At one time it was thought that zander only took small lures (and indeed, small baits), but I've had too many on big lures to know that it isn't flukey at all. It was my friend Colin Hall who first put me on to catching zander on big Bulldawgs on the troll. I now know that the same or similar big rubber jobs will take zander from the bank too: it's just a bit less like hard work from a boat. Now surely these Bulldawgs ain't a lot like the zanders' food fish, are they? Maybe I need to rethink that issue; it could be that early experiences have built up a prejudice in me. I have no doubt at all that there's a great deal to learn about zander on lures, but you can be confident that they do work well, whether it's in a big deep river or reservoir, or a shallow Fenland drain or a Midlands canal. Don't fish without a wire trace though; zander don't mind them and all zander waters have pike in them.

11 Game Fishing: Salmon

By Dave Steuart

The first thing to understand when trying to catch salmon is that they don't eat in freshwater; they cannot, their stomachs won't allow it so you're on a loser to start with. Having grasped this fact one can appreciate that it is factors other than necessity to eat that cause a salmon to take hold of spinner, plug, fly, worm, prawn or whatever, whether it be a predatory reflex action, aggressiveness, territorial assertion, or downright stupidity. Our non-migratory species, will, when in feeding mood, eat a variety of foods and, depending upon quantity, the tiniest food forms to the largest they can swallow. Although conditions affect their feeding patterns to a certain extent, they have got to eat sometime and so are then vulnerable to the angler. The returning 'prodigals', however, fat with excesses from 'overseas' and with their stomach atrophied, have to be induced to take a bait (bait in this context means a spinner of whatever type is being used) by the application of a well-known general procedure, based on the experiences of the past and present experts of the written word and aligned to one's own lore.

This generally accepted basic set of rules is closely allied to water temperatures, for the obvious reason that the metabolism of all fish is tied to this, and in this respect a salmon is no different to any other fish. When the water is cold, and the salmon's metabolic rate is low, it has neither the inclination nor the energy to move far for a bait and so the salmon angler endeavours to present his bait as close as possible to the fish, at eye level. As the water warms and a salmon becomes capable of greater energy, the angler fishes higher in the water and generally a little faster.

The well-known temperature of 48°F, which most salmon fly fishermen use as a guide to decide whether to fish near the surface with a floating line, or deeper with a sunk line, can also be used as a guide by the

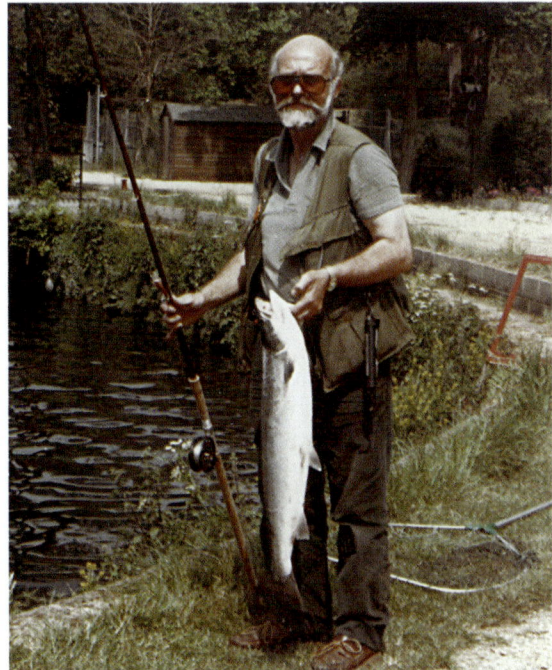

David Lincoln Steuart with a nice salmon from the River Itchen, using paternoster and centre pin. (Photograph courtesy of Dave Steuart)

The legendary Kay Steuart with a bag of grilse taken on Mepps. (Photograph courtesy of Dave Steuart)

spinning man to change his style or manner of presenting his bait. Some salmon fishers tend to use one method for the whole season and doubtless lose some possible chances of a fish because of it.

There are reasons other than temperature, of course, for fishing with a certain size or type of spinner in a certain way and I will elaborate on these by explaining why I use a particular method and bait as we explore the field of 'spinning for salmon'.

You cannot catch fish if you're not fishing where they are, so it is as well to familiarize yourself with the current speeds and river-bed contours where salmon like to rest while awaiting the conditions to urge them to move upstream. They generally like to lie in fast water, or appear to, in similar conditions to those one would associate with barbel swims. I say 'appear to',

as I have perceived that although a salmon is at first glance lying in fast, strong water, it is usually positioned where a division of current or turbulence creates backflow, an easier flow in which the fish can maintain its position. This can be seen when particles of detritus are travelling with the flow and the behaviour of such matter is observed as it enters the salmon's 'lie'. However, as a generalization, we look for salmon where the water flows fast.

The obvious lies therefore are the outside of bends, where the river flows strong and deep – in our southern rivers, this is often where piles have been hammered to contain the river by arresting bank erosion; deep-cut banks caused by fast currents; narrow stretches creating a speeding-up of flow; and gradients. Fish like to lie just upstream of a gradient where there is a pull over their backs as the flow accelerates, influenced by the increased velocity down the incline. Sometimes it is the tail of a pool, at other times the 'run-in' to a pool. Dictated by the angle of the gradient, fish may or may not lie in the water flowing over them. It may be too fast, too turbulent and without obstruction to create short-rest lies, as some rocky waterfalls give to ascending fish.

The pool below a gradient will hold fish in various places, dependent upon its character. There could be fish lying alongside the main flow into the pool: if it is deep, they might lie in a back-current underneath the white water where it enters the pool, and not always near the bottom, alienating to flow. If the flow enters to one side of the pool they may lie at the current's edge or alongside the bank edge – smooth rock faces, piling, or straight-cut banking, and will lie at all depths between the river bed and surface alongside these, again the depth at which they lie being subject to a flow to their liking.

Cover is important. Salmon will sometimes prefer lying in shallow water where there

Static or slowly worked paternoster system for salmon spinning. The lure can be a minnow or a bar spoon, spoon or plug.

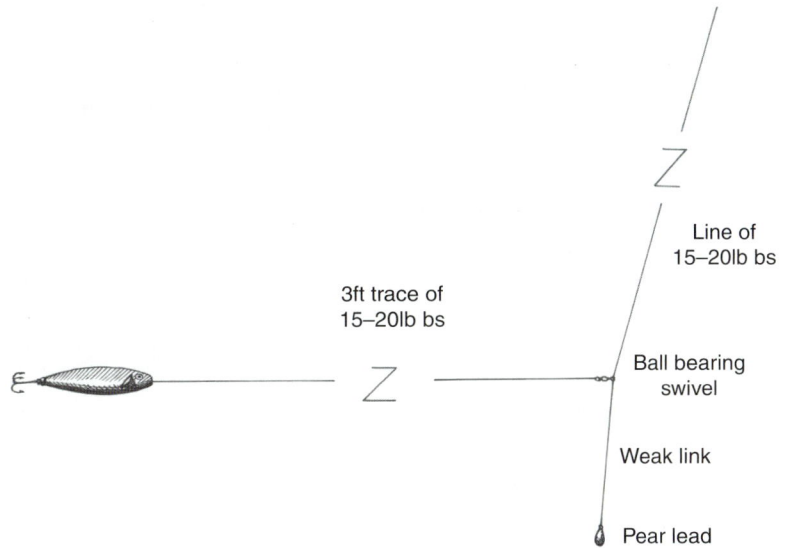

Line of
15–20lb bs

3ft trace of
15–20lb bs

Ball bearing
swivel

Weak link

Pear lead

is cover, rather than in deep water where conditions would cause them to be easily visible, for example slow flows and gin-clear water. High banks will give cover, as will trees, bridges and any overhang. Remove the cover, as some misinformed anglers and fishery administrators are inclined to do, and you remove the fish. Groynes generally create the conditions that fish like and such features should be recognizable even to the novice. One very important consideration, when spinning for salmon or any other fish – keep out of sight of the fish.

It's about time we did some fishing.

Dave Steuart playing a salmon at the Boards swim at Abbey Mill fishery. (Photograph courtesy of Dave Steuart)

Paternoster Spinning

Early season fishing for 'springers' can be a hard, cold, fruitless job, but, if successful, the prize is so great that all the effort and discomfort becomes well worthwhile. In my view, there is no other fish so beautiful and symmetrically perfect as a white-bellied, silver-flanked, steel-blue-backed spring salmon. I live in the south, near London, and the nearest salmon fishing available to me is the River Test, the Hampshire Avon and the Dorset Stour. All these rivers are fairly fast-flowing and gravel-bottomed, so when fishing for the few springers that still enter these rivers, from the opening day of 1 February for a couple of months or so, I favour spinning paternoster fashion, for reasons that I will explain later. This is a fairly simple way of fishing a bait very close to the river bed, a bait that travels very slowly through the spring lies.

Basically, terminal tackle is simple. The chosen line, 15–20lb breaking strain, is tied to a ball-ring swivel; a nylon trace approximately 3ft long of the same strength as the line is attached to the other end of the swivel and to the trace is tied a link swivel to attach the bait of your choice. From the top-eye of the ball-bearing swivel a 6–10in length of nylon hangs, of much lighter bs in case it gets snagged (I favour 6lb bs), and to this nylon I tie a link for the easy changing of pear leads.

During the course of a day's fishing the pear lead size may be altered several times to counteract different pressures on the line of current speed and depth, which would cause a bait to travel too fast across the river, too high in the water, or, in the case of too heavy a lead, not to travel across by the current's pressure on the line, but remain anchored. Lead size is all-important; don't be afraid of it. In some lies in heavy water you sometimes need 2oz or more.

The method of fishing is to cast across the river in a downstream direction at an angle of about 45 degrees. Line is allowed to flow from the spool to shoot the lead to the 'bottom', the bail is closed (fixed spool reel) or the gears engaged (multiplier) and, with the rod held high, the tackle travels in an arc from its cast position to the near bank as the current pushes on the across-stream line, lead and bait. The further downstream one casts and the higher the rod is held, the slower the tackle will travel across, but avoid casting too far down – a very long line will make hook penetration more difficult.

If the lead size is right one can feel it dragging the bottom as it comes over; if it occasionally catches, a slight lift of the rod will free it to continue its journey. When the tackle reaches the angler's bank, it is rewound, the angler takes a few steps downstream, then recasts. By this method, the river is searched methodically yard after yard in the hope of putting the bait very close to the fish, right on the bottom,

One for the bank – on Mepps spinner. (Photograph courtesy of Dave Steuart)

for, as mentioned above, when the water is cold, as it is in the early season, a salmon has neither the inclination nor the energy to chase a bait far or fast.

Salmon will enter a river readily enough in water at almost freezing point, 33°F, especially on a spring tide, then will move slowly upriver until confronted by an obstruction such as a weir, waterfall or any gradient that is steep enough to cause white water. In the cold water they haven't the energy to surmount difficult water, so if one is lucky enough to be able to fish the lower beats in early spring – especially the first major obstacles – before the water temperature rises to approximately 10°F above freezing, there should be a few new fish waiting to be caught by correct bait presentation. After the water reaches the low 'forties', fish will start negotiating falls and will move upstream at a faster pace.

So we hope we are fishing water where early salmon have reached; we are using the paternoster method as we know we must get down to the fish and fish slowly; and as fish may be very scarce we know we must search the 'ground' thoroughly, but what of baits? There are several considerations here and if we start with the salmon we realize that in its cold state it needs a jolt, a high impact to cause a reaction, and so we start with size and use a large bait. We must then consider the water in which the salmon is lying. Is it clear or dirty, deep or shallow? We assume it is going to be fairly heavy, fast water in February/March, the time of rains and melting snows, so we also take notice of that in our bait assessment.

Assuming rains have made the river a bit coloured, along with the large bait we will also need a bright colour in order to attract the salmon's attention. The Avon favourite is yellow; in Devon minnows, the yellow-belly; and in heavy, coloured conditions, I would use a 3½in bait. There is nothing to beat a light wooden or plastic Devon

for paternoster work. Any heavy metal job fished by the method would soon catch the bottom and snag; the wooden Devon, however, in any situation where the current eases, instead of fishing deeper will float up and keep clear. Plastic patterns, Dibro Devon minnows, for example, need such little flow to keep them working that they rarely ever snag. Without wooden or plastic Devons we couldn't fish a *short*-link paternoster with the bait only a few inches from the river bed, following the contours. As the depth increases, the lead takes down the bait; as it shallows, the lead bounces up the slope with the bait following instead of catching up.

In very dirty water the big 3½in yellow-belly is necessary even in shallow rivers, to give enough impact, whereas in shallow water of 3ft or less, with just a touch of colour, I would either change down to a 2½in yellow-belly, or change the colour and retain the large size brown/gold, black/gold – a 3½in yellow-belly would be just too much on shallows and might put a fish off. In deeper water with only a little colour, it would be as well to use the large size and bright colour while temperatures are low, as even slight turbidity causes a deterioration in visibility the deeper it gets.

In gin-clear water – and we've found this at the beginning of the season once or twice in recent years – I would still take my first consideration as read and start with a large bait, but a brown/gold, or black/gold wooden Devon, or a natural sprat, a golden sprat, or what I call my kipper-Devon. Natural sprats are soft, but mounted on a spinning flight (a celluloid-vaned flight is light enough to be used paternoster fashion). They catch salmon *and* they smell nice – golden sprat catches a lot of fish but I've never liked the smell much, although deformalizing might help in this direction. I've tried smoked sprat – they look fine and smell okay, but break up. As a change, I have recently been using my 'kipper-Devon'. This is simply a celluloid-vaned flight with a Devon-shaped length of cork glued to the mounting-pin. The cork is made slim to allow a wrapping of skin, taken from the flank of a lovely golden kipper. It is kept in place by a winding of elastic cotton. The skin, shading from blue-black to golden, can be wrapped in such a way as to give the bait a dark back and golden belly. It's a Devon that smells nice and when a fish takes hold, perhaps tastes nice. The cork body gives it buoyancy to fish paternoster style.

As the water warms – getting into the low forties – it is usually clearer and with the fish a little livelier we cut down the bait size to 2½in, lengthen the lead-link a few inches to fish the bait a little above the salmon, while decreasing the lead size slightly so that the bait fishes across a mite faster. Bait colour is sober. However, despite the salmon's slightly increased liveliness, if the river is still very coloured we return to the early method of using big bait, perhaps 3in instead of 3½in – yellow-belly, shorter lead-link and fish very slowly. This is not so much for high impact, but to give the fish a chance to see the bait.

Later in the spring, when water temperatures are in the upper forties, we may dispense with the paternoster altogether and fish a different method, but will always return to it after heavy rains, when conditions dictate that we again have to put the bait right into the salmon's mouth.

A further point about fishing the paternoster when temperatures have reached the low forties and rising, and the water is clear, is that we can start to increase the number of steps between casts. The fish will see a bait from a greater distance and when in taking mood will be prepared to move further to intercept it or chase it, and so we can work through the river much faster. We can also confine ourselves to fishing the

obvious lies that are appearing as the river levels drop – they're not always so easily read when the river is high and when a fish could turn up anywhere. Going through faster, plus the lengthening of daylight, will mean that we have time to work through a pool twice; the second time through will sometimes produce a fish. Probably first time through woke it up and second time decided its interest.

I favour the paternoster and the light Devons as the method for early season for many reasons. It fishes slowly; it takes the bait right down to the fish; if the lead gets snagged the weak lead-link will break and the bait is retained; the bait rarely gets snagged; in the fast water of early season the Devon does not create drag and increase speed as it comes across; the Devon commences fishing as soon as it enters the water; being buoyant, the Devon will spin even if the lead is allowed to act as an anchor to hold the bait in one position for a known difficult fish; the Devon will fish right under the far bank by allowing the lead to shoot to the bottom upon entry, before the current acts on the line and brings it across. In sum, this method is the easiest way to present a bait correctly in the early season. When fish are scarce it can also be the most boring and *is* tiring – what I call 'the hard flog of spring salmon fishing'.

Orthodox Spinning

Unfortunately (or fortunately, depending upon how you look at it), it is not possible to use the paternoster in all rivers. In turbulent, rocky rivers, both small and large, which are much associated with salmon fishing, it is not practical to fish with a hanging lead, unless you own a lead mine, for it will continually be getting snagged. One then fishes in a far more orthodox fashion with up-trace lead, Wye lead or

Jardine lead, and fishes as deep as possible consistent with keeping the tackle from getting snagged. I still favour the wooden or plastic Devons and apply all the foregoing lore as to bait size, colour, and so on, but some anglers who know their rivers very well will use a heavy metal Devon, with or without up-trace lead as conditions demand, knowing just how deep they can allow it to go and just where to raise it out of trouble. The knowledge probably cost them dear at first. With the wooden Devon, if the lead is felt to touch bottom or rock, a slight lift to clear it should also lift the Devon out of trouble.

The method of fishing is still across and down, trying to cover as much holding water as possible. I have the feeling that, were it possible, the paternoster would outfish the orthodox in early season, although many hundreds of fish fall to the latter method. Compared to the rivers where we can fish paternoster-style, the others hold so many fish that sooner or later any method of bait presentation is bound to pass near a fish willing to take.

Long spoons and bar spoons can be used to fish salmon early season in shallow streams by making a fairly long cast downstream, to fish them across as slow as possible. The trouble arises when trying to get them to go deep, especially bar spoons. They create such a pull when fished downstream that, unless very heavily leaded, they fish close to the surface. Such spoons are best left until the water warms up, when they can be fished in a different manner.

With river temperatures in the upper forties we can start on more interesting ways of spinning providing the water is a good colour – clear or just slightly coloured. With a slight colour we might still fish paternoster-style, but make our casts at a lesser angle downstream so that it will fish round faster. In clear water, we can dispense with the link-lead and fish in a more

orthodox manner with up-trace leads to Devons, Toby spoons, bar spoons, wobbling spoons, plugs – anything that the angler thinks might interest a fish. Sizes of Devons will have dropped to 2–2½in, while other baits will range about that size, with wobbling spoons and plugs perhaps just slightly larger. Bar spoons, with their greater vibration impact, can be a little smaller, although I personally will still use, say, a Mepp no. 5 Aglia in the Avon or Stour where the fish run large. On the River Test, though, I will drop to a size 4 during the same period, for the salmon are a few pounds lighter, so there we have yet another consideration factor in choice of bait size.

We might fish a few square casts so that the bait travels across as we wind back, controlling the fishing depth by rod angle and winding speed, with the bait coming across slightly downstream and making an inviting turn as we wind when the bait has come three-quarters of the way across to the angler's bank.

Once temperatures have reached the fifties I will fish some of the day with

A handsome fellow, in April 2007. And the fish too.

Mepps or similar bar spoons in preference to other baits, and do a deal of casting slightly upstream, winding back so that the bait comes across square to the current with the blade giving a broader image to the upstream-facing fish. Small rivers must be approached very carefully when adopting this method, as the fish will be opposite you in the river and so any careless movement on the bank or in the water, although it may not always frighten the fish away, will make them nervous and unlikely to take a bait.

Upstream Spinning

Providing the water is clear, the low fifties are also the river temperatures when I have the occasional throw directly upstream in fast water, winding back fairly rapidly. Although some anglers are under the impression that a fish has to move fast to take a bait coming downstream at speed, it is a fallacy, as it in fact requires less effort from the fish than the taking of a bait just dangled in the fast water. The fish, seeing the bait coming down, may move its position slightly and simply intercept it with little effort, but even if it chases the bait downstream, no extra energy is required. If we assume the fast water is travelling at 4mph and a speed of 1mph is required to work the bar spoon, to make it revolve we must wind at a speed in excess of 5mph. But a fish travelling with the current has only to swim at a little over 1mph to overtake the bait as the current takes it downstream. To take a bait dangled in the current it must swim a little more than the current speed.

Come the summer and low water conditions, very much more of my spinning is then directly upstream. There are, in my opinion, lots of advantages to be had by fishing in this manner, which increase as the summer advances. One of them, and a very important one where salmon are concerned, is that I seem to have a more successful number of landings to takes. I have always had a few salmon come adrift during the course of a season, and every salmon angler I know has similar experiences, but casting up and winding down increases the chance of a hook taking a fair hold.

If a salmon intercepts the bait as it comes down, the hook should lodge in a corner of its mouth; if it follows down and turns back as it takes, which salmon often do, the hold should also be in the scissors. This is a very secure hook-hold, although the 'kiting' effect of such a hold on a large, long-jawed, cock fish can be a little disconcerting.

When a fish is hooked, the downstream angler is already in a better position for

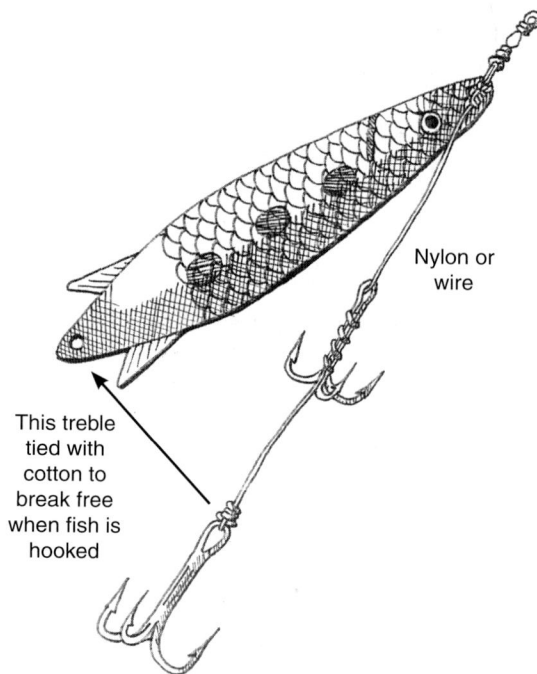

Nylon or wire

This treble tied with cotton to break free when fish is hooked

A very good way of fishing a Toby-style spoon in salmon fishing. Twin trebles help with the hooking of salmon that take the lure crossways on.

playing it from below, when compared to the angler who hooks a fish from upstream. The salmon will often take off upriver, which gives the downstream angler the advantage of having the fish fighting the current as well as himself. If weeds have grown, there is less fear of entanglement in playing a fish from below; if weeds are abundant, it is often advisable to cast up and spin down the runs between them when it is not possible to fish downstream. If cut weed is coming down, providing it isn't too much, it is also feasible to get a few casts in by throwing upstream and winding down with the stuff.

Another advantage is that as the current bears upon the line, one can cast a longish line upstream to the far bank and spin down that bank a long way before the bait leaves it and starts coming across. And because the bait will come down in a fairly straight line it is a very quick way of covering a lot of water; by casting up alongside the lies the bait must have been seen by, and be in close proximity to, all the fish. The depth at which the bait is fished can also be fairly easily controlled.

In the low fifties, I use a Mepp size 4, or 3 if very clear, with Devons of ½–2in, and as I concentrate more on upstream work towards and during summer, I will have dropped to a Mepp 2. Should I feel like a change, I use metal Devons for their ease in casting without up-trace lead. In very low water even a tiny 1in Devon or no. 1 or 0 Mepp will take fish. These small baits can be cast to a fish several times without worrying it unduly.

Over the last couple of years when upstream spinning, if fishing a small bar spoon where I have needed lead to aid casting, or to fish it deeper, I have placed the lead right down near the spinner to act as a head for the bait – like a Voblex. I have fished this way since having a hell of a pull when winding down fast, but not

connecting. As I finished the retrieve I saw a salmon swimming down directly behind the up-trace lead and it occurred to me that on occasions when I have had a pull and not hooked the fish, it could well be a fish that hit the up-trace lead. When casting up and retrieving a bait and using an up-trace lead, the first thing the fish sees is the lead and if it's really in a taking mood, it may well hit the lead before the following spinner. The trouble is, it rarely gives one a second chance.

It will be noticed that as the temperature of the river has risen through the year, so we have used smaller baits, fished higher in the water and faster. As fish become livelier through the year, so they will refuse larger baits, or even be frightened by them. I don't pretend to understand this, but have observed fish that have refused a bait, been rested, then taken a smaller one. Although I have caught salmon by continually casting to them with small baits, quite often continually showing them a large bait will cause them to move house.

There are many observations one can make about salmon taking spinning baits. For example, fresh run fish will sometimes take a larger bait of fish that have been in the river for a while, and yet, towards the autumn, stale fish may well start hitting large baits again. In the latter case it could be an aggressiveness that becomes positive as the spawning season nears commencement, as I have watched cock salmon chasing trout and salmon parr off the redds during cutting.

Small Rivers

Fishing some of the smaller, natural rocky rivers, often with heavily bushed and tree-lined banks, does tend to cut down on one's ability to cover all the water where a fish might rest, but then such waters are

99

usually fairly easy to read and the salmon lies rather obvious. It may be that there are only one or two stances from which to fish a stretch of water; covering it as well as possible will therefore require upstream, downstream and square casting, all from one position. This may mean adding or removing lead to cast to a new position and to fish at the right depth and speed – not so critical later in the year in the small river, but important early in the season. This, I think, is why so many of the locals prefer worming – an art if fished well and more certain of fishing right.

Some of the casting must be very accurate in streams. When trying to place a bait into a small gap amid or beneath foliage on the far bank, it can be all too easy to find the cast snagged up in the surrounding foliage on your own side of the bank. Such pinpoint casting is much easier when all the weight is in one place – at the end of the line – so either use baits with sufficient weight 'built in', or place the lead close to it, as I have suggested for upstream fishing. Some anglers like heavy metal Devons for this sort of work and catch a lot of fish on them too.

Temperature changes affect the fish of small streams more readily than in the larger rivers, as such changes can happen more quickly. A large river is less likely to be affected by a small change in air temperature, but the lesser volume of a stream may well be affected enough to stop fish taking, or to start them showing an interest.

Hooking

I once saw three salmon holding station over 8ft of water. They were only some 3ft below the surface, sitting comfortably on top of a backflow, although the current over their backs was fast and strong. I flicked a Devon upstream of them, watched it come flickering downstream past them and saw the smallest of the three, a fish about 7lb, swing out and follow the Devon. As it swung round into the slack water, the salmon closed its mouth over the lure. I did nothing except continue winding, expecting to feel the rod go down, but in the same second as it took the bait the salmon opened its mouth and the Devon came out spinning. I didn't feel a thing. The fish turned back to lie with the other two and showed no further interest. Although I intermittently tried various baits during the course of the day, all three fish took no notice, although in the evening the seven-pounder did take a prawn. Pity about the other two. One was 20lb and the other about 14lb.

I have seen salmon swim up to the bait and knock it with their nose but with their mouth shut. I mention this and the previous instance to show that there can be problems with hooking salmon. Occasionally, one gets a very sharp knock as a bait comes across; I often wonder if it is a warning to the intruder to keep away and whether a salmon does it with its mouth closed. It always excites me anyway, as another cast to the same spot often results in a proper take.

The main difficulty lies in the strength of a salmon's jaw, for, as in nearly all animals, the jaw muscles are the strongest. When a salmon takes hold of a bait and the angler strikes, I don't think he moves it within the fish's mouth at all and so doesn't drive in the hooks. Instead, the salmon feels the pull, opens its mouth and ejects the lot. When fishing down and across early in the season, and the salmon hasn't moved far for the bait and is probably still facing upstream while holding the bait, a good hook-hold is least likely. Later in the season when one is fishing square, faster or upstream, when a salmon moves further to a bait and then turns back to its lie, a good hook-hold is much more on the cards.

Some experts say that you should never strike, but let the weight of the fish set the hook, as it will turn away if it doesn't feel a pull. Some anglers I know use very stiff rods and strike hard. I've tried both methods, but still fish fall off. Probably a delayed hard pull is best, but a quicker strike can be better in summer when grilse are running – fish which are lively and eject a bait quickly.

Another problem is caused by the long-bait Devon, Toby, and so on, especially early in the season or in dirty water when one is using large sizes. I'm positive that salmon often take hold crosswise and with only a treble at the tail, the hook therefore isn't within the mouth of the fish. I have got over this problem a little by adding a centre-treble to some of my Devons and spoons, but in a manner that still allows the Devon to slide up the line out of the salmon's mouth when the fish is hooked and for the spoon to swing free. A Devon or spoon that remains in a hooked salmon's jaw may be waggled about in an effort to get rid of it, with the result that the hooks are levered out.

If one is prepared to go the trouble of replacing baits that continual casting will destroy, one way of overcoming the hooking difficulties to some extent is to use natural baits whenever possible. Natural sprat and a hard strike rarely result in a missed fish, as the soft bait doesn't stop the hooks moving when the strike is made. Golden sprat will last longer, as the formalin preservative toughens the flesh, but hooks can still be struck through it.

When a small bait is wanted, a natural minnow makes a good spinning bait. I haven't yet used it much for salmon, but have caught a lot of trout with it. Some old-time anglers have taken pretty hefty bags of salmon with natural minnow, so I guess it's only the modern angler's terrific choice of baits that has caused it to fall out of favour. I was planning to fish it hard back in 1976, but with the drought conditions there weren't any fish to throw it at.

There are times when a fresh, lively salmon will hammer into a bait with terrific enthusiasm, hooking itself solidly. They have smashed into floats, or when I have been retrieving them along the surface on days when I've been coarse fishing. Such suicidal fish are rare, unfortunately, but knowing they will sometimes have a go at a surface bait wound upstream did give me the idea of trotting a spinner to a difficult lie and retrieving slowly back. I have caught one or two fish like this. One was caught where the high but sloping bank made me very obviously visible when I cast to fish, so a spinner was trotted and retrieved, a good fish took and was landed. Another angler, seeing the float from a distance, thought the fish was caught on worm. I didn't enlighten him.

But back to this hooking business. Remember that when spinning, the length of line is ever changing and, should you strike, you must strike very hard on a long line, but a lot less hard on a short one, especially so on the latter when fishing lighter tackle in low water conditions. And don't fish with the rod pointing down the line, or a really hard take may cause tackle failure.

Things to be wary of when a salmon is hooked is head shaking. The salmon thumps the rod like hell, which can loosen the hook-hold. This frightens me to death if it's a big fish. I always ease pressure when this happens; the fish usually stops and then goes off on a long run. Another time that the hook-hold may give is when a fish explodes from the water, but as this is usually the termination of a run the angler will not be holding hard anyway, so there's little that can be done – unless one believes in the power of prayer.

Playing a Salmon

A salmon is often a big fish. It is also strong, fast and acrobatic. It often likes to move around a lot, relieving the angler of a considerable amount of line in the process. This last aspect is one thing that novice anglers don't really appreciate; that it is always best to keep a fish on as short a line as possible. If a fish takes off downstream – get off after it. If it takes off upstream – get off after it. The more line you lose from the reel, the longer it will take to get the fish back into a controllable position.

Now I don't mean by that last remark that if a big fish takes off you should hang on hard – that's the last thing you should do even with heavy tackle, for either the hook will tear out or break, the line will break, or something equally disastrous will happen. What you should do is chase the fish upstream or down, letting as little line off the reel as you can and retrieving it as you get near. With a fish that's run downstream, pass it by and get below it, for you should try to play a big fish from downstream of it.

The foregoing is fine for clear banks, but what of obstructed banks? Sometimes the obstructions can be traversed, or trees can be passed by taking the rod around; the river may be shallow enough to wade round and, if you a have a companion, marvels can be accomplished. All this is necessary when a fish runs down, but not so if a fish goes up, as (unless it goes around a bend) the angler can usually get the fish back from below, since the fish is fighting both current and angler. If the bank is clear, however, as I said in the beginning, get off after it.

What if a big fish has gone a long way down and the obstructions are impassable? You can try pumping it up if you are restricted in either direction, but if the bank upstream is open, walk the fish up. When the fish has finished its downward rush and turned to face the current, wind tight, clamp your hand upon the reel drum and walk upriver. The fish will usually come up with you without fuss so long as you keep the pressure steady. Walk it up as far as you think necessary, or as far as you can go, then walk down, retrieving line until you are opposite the fish or have to repeat the procedure. The fish may go down again and you may have to go 'walkies' a lot before eventually winning the day.

The first thing I do if I hook a salmon of any size upstream of a bridge, sluice, obstructed bank, or anywhere that I cannot follow down, is to walk the fish up well away from trouble if at all feasible. I feel a lot happier and in a much more masterful position once I've done that. If a fish has gone down and you cannot get it back, there are still a few courses open. You can let out all the line from the reel and send a companion down to try to cast across it. If he is successful, cut your line, go down and re-tie. If you are on your own and possess a spare reel or spool of line, you can let off the line, tie it to a tree, go down with the rod and reel fitted with the spare line, cast and pick up the original line, try to gain some slack, then cut and tie to the new stuff. You can look for a largish tree branch (not waterlogged), tie your line to it, chuck it well out and hope to pick it up below with the fish still attached – or you can go swimming. Rather you than me.

Salmon play pretty fair as a rule. They don't dive into weeds and snags, unless they are stale fish that have learnt the area. One place I fished last season, where because of the low water the new fish became potted, they used to disappear during the day beneath an old turbine house in dead, slack water. When they came out in the evening, a fish hooked would belt straight back underneath.

Anglers will always argue amiably. When using a fixed spool reel, Barrie often recommends back-pedalling to a running fish, but I disagree. It may be adequate to play some fish this way, but I personally don't like it for fast-moving fish like game fish, or when fishing with very fine lines. The reels are not balanced to revolve fast through the gears and one gets a 'rock' action when a fish is bolting. I admit that to play a fish from the clutch it is essential to have a reel with an ultra-smooth clutch, with no high spots, but there are such models and regular servicing to keep them so is entirely up to the angler.

After a big fish has been landed that has taken a lot of line, remove the terminal tackle and let the loose line flow freely downstream from the spool. This will remove the kinks put in the line by the drum revolving as the fish ran. It is a good idea to do this on any reel occasionally, for the line well down a spool will become crimped due to the line pressure above.

Tackle

As we have just talked of fixed spool reels, I will mention reels before rods. There are only two types worth bothering with when salmon spinning and they are the fixed spool reel and the multiplier. I occasionally spin with a centre pin, but that is just the whim of a fool – the other two types are far more efficient for the job. If you are only interested in purchasing one model, buy a large fixed spool reel, but if you are going to fish the season through you will require two models; as a comparison, a Mitchell 300 and a Mitchell 306, or their modern equivalents.

For big fish, an open river and heavy lines, the multiplier is nicer to use and is my choice. It is easy to cast with despite the talk of overruns. However, it is easier to cast with a fixed spool reel in awkward places, such as rocky, tree-lined rivers. Where

following is not possible, heavy tackle is necessary even if the fish are not over-large. In these sorts of rivers, as mentioned previously, it is essential to be able to place a bait into little holes between branches, under foliage, and so on. A reel needs to carry at least 100yd of 15–20lb breaking strain for these conditions, though I would prefer it to carry 150–200yd. For the open river with runs of big fish, a reel that will hold the same sort of lengths and breaking strains is ideal.

For summer and upstream work, when a river is less strong and the fish are smaller, where I am casting light baits and where I have no fear of losses, a Mitchell 300 or modern equivalent, loaded with 8–12lb bs, is ample. I often fish very much lighter than that, only half the recommended bs, but 10lb bs is what I would recommend for summer salmon.

With big fish like salmon I work out first what line strength is sensible to give me a fair chance of success and, along with other factors, the rod and reel are dictated by that. For heavy lines on the big river, a double-handed 10ft job would be fine, though would be too awkward on a little river, in which case a single-handed, strong eight or nine footer, capable of handling the same line strength, would be a better proposition. For summer work, a medium-action eight to nine footer, coupled to the 10lb line, gives an angler a deal of fun. Salmon are often full of fight in the warmer water and create hell – and heaven – for the angler. I don't apologize for not giving the reader of this chapter much information on the multitude of spinning baits available and their uses. I consider it more important to know something about the fish and its behaviour to the size of bait and the manner in which it is fished at different times of the year. As yet, there is no infallible spinning bait; and if I had one, I wouldn't tell you.

Editor's Note

The above was written some time ago by Dave Steuart, but he confirms that he wouldn't change it in any way. However, the regulations mean that one has to be very careful these days about spinning for salmon and, in a letter written in March 2007, Dave provided me with his thoughts on the modern scene. He indicated that he would fish in exactly the same way now as he had done years earlier, if he was allowed to. Dave argued that it was not the methods that are at fault but, as he saw it, the bureaucracy within the Environment Agency (EA), which has introduced inappropriate by-laws concerning fishing methods. In his letter he stated that 'On the Test one is only allowed to spin or fly fish until 16 June and all salmon caught must be returned. Fine. I don't mind returning them as we stopped killing salmon here back in 1990, but as all fish must be returned I do not see why we are not allowed to fish with better methods when the river is out of sorts, except worms which anglers tend to let salmon swallow.' He went on to say that the EA by-laws meant that after 16 June '... you can kill as many as you can catch and you can then also use any method you like. So one is restricted how to catch them when legally bound to return them, but can do what you like when you can kill them.' Dave argued that this made no sense because '... in heavy, dirty water, fly, and sometimes spinner, is pretty hopeless. The by-law is there for one reason only, to try to make sure you don't catch many, or any.'

In the Wessex region, on the Avon and Stour, it is made even more difficult. One may fly fish only until 15 May, after which it is no holds barred. Again, the fishing has been made as difficult as possible for spring salmon fishing. Of course, a few fish will be caught on 'fly', if the heavy tubes and sunk lines can be called fly fishing but, as all genuine anglers return salmon to those rivers now, there should not be such rules.

12 Game Fishing: Trout

By Fred J. Taylor

Editor's Note

The logic and philosophy propounded by Fred J. in the chapter following is in my view unassailable, although there will, of course, be some who may not agree. His approach has been much my own and I can confirm, for example, his experiences on the tiny trout waters where a fly rod would be a near impossibility. Bill Winship and I used to fish such waters in North Yorkshire, simply by asking the farmers, and we had wonderful sport on tiny bar spoons. Fish of over half a pound were unusual, but we did get some nice ones. We would retain a few small fish for a meal, but most went back after careful handling.

There is more scope for the trout spinner on some of the big waters, such as the Scottish waters, which hold ferox. My own biggest brownie came from Loch Lomond and weighed exactly 16lb. From the opposite bank of a bay we'd seen something striking at frogs and toads as they swam in amongst sparsely spaced reed and rush steps. So we drifted the boat across and from about 60yd away I fired a plug at the area. I chose a yellow Gudebrod Sniper about 4in long, because I felt it looked a bit like a frog. It was taken first cast and a mighty battle ensued. The big fish was returned alive and well to the water.

Elsewhere I've had big brownies casting spinners from the bank, such as a 5¾lb fish from a rock-strewn shore of Lough Corrib. That fish took a small Toby spoon.

On common-or-garden Norwich spoons I've had rainbows to 7¼lb and even a few decent fish to spinnerbaits. On Ardingly reservoir in southern England I had permission from the fishery owner to use any method for the trout, and I caught some good rainbows trolling minnows fast and

Barrie with his best trout, a ferox of 16lb from Loch Lomond, on a yellow Gudebrod Sniper which looked like the frogs the fish was chasing. Hugh Reynolds looks on.

shallow, plus some good browns trolling small Tobys fast and deep. All the fish I have mentioned were returned to the water. Now read on for an authoritative account by Fred J.

Still Waters

The late, great master fly fisherman Oliver Kite is reputed to have referred to still-water trout fishing as 'spinning with a fly rod'. If he did (which I doubt), he was almost certainly referring to that branch of still-water trouting which involves the casting and retrieving of flies dressed to look like minnows or the fry of other species. Oliver Kite was also credited with those immortal words, 'Chuck it out, pull it back and when you can't, you've got one.' If he did, in fact, make such a remark (and I'm sure he did), he was obviously referring to the use of the above-mentioned lure-type flies.

I would hesitate to disagree with Oliver Kite, and on matters etymological I would

not do so at all, but there is more to lure fishing for trout than he would have had us believe. True, if you do no more than chuck-it-out-and-pull-it-back, you'll catch trout often enough to regard it as a reasonably effective method. But, although the casting of lure flies with a fly rod and traditional fly tackle requires a degree of skill, it does not take too long to reach a state of reasonable efficiency. Having cast the lure, however, the speed and manner of its retrieve probably require a little more than the sheer mechanical expertise needed for casting. Which is why, generally speaking, the fly-only ruling applied to most still-water trout fisheries borders on the ridiculous.

If we accept the fact that 'flies' tied to represent small fish are strictly lures, and if lures, as suggested elsewhere in this book, are objects that flutter, spin, wobble or move in a manner attractive to bigger fish, why should we not be allowed to present those flies with a spinning rod and a casting reel? Most of the trout fishing available to the average angler today is conducted on

Leslie Robbins with a Lake District ferox of 15¼lb. (Photograph courtesy of Gordon Burton)

Gordon on Loch Awe with a ferox of 14¼lb caught on a Darter jerkbait at 35ft, using a lead-cored line. (Photograph courtesy of Gordon Burton)

a daily permit, put-and-take basis. Waters are stocked, bag limits imposed, records kept and generally speaking it all works very well.

But why, I wonder, do public bodies controlling vast acreages of trout water which they claim to be 'open to the public', almost invariably enforce the fly-only rule? They have stocked their waters with trout and now advertise the fact that they have, this year, introduced X number of browns and Y number of rainbows averaging so many pounds or parts of a pound apiece. They seek to attract the customers, to collect the revenue, to give sport to those who like to catch trout, to run and maintain good fisheries, and yet, despite their claims to be 'open to the public', they cater only for a small minority of the anglers in this country.

What of the angler who has no fly rod, no desire to purchase one and neither the wish nor time to learn the basics of fly casting? There is no way he can fish these so-called public waters because for some obscure reason his spinning tackle is strictly taboo.

It so happens that I do have a great deal of fly tackle and despite the fact that I am not an expert fly fisher, I manage to catch my fair share of trout each season. What's more, I enjoy it, and to my way of thinking that's what fishing is all about, whatever the species. But not everyone enjoys fly fishing and there are many situations where more pleasure could be achieved from the use of other tackle were it allowed. For the life of me, I cannot figure out why spinning should not be allowed on all these public waters.

I've been told a hundred reasons of course. Fly fishers have argued emotionally but quite illogically about 'sporting methods' and 'unsporting methods', and I've listened to passionate outbursts from time to time about so-called 'unsporting tackle'. But I wonder. How can a method or a piece of tackle be sporting or unsporting? Only at the hands of someone who is not himself a sportsman can a method or a piece of tackle be put to an unsporting use. (Even a leister is not unsporting if it's propped up against a tree.) [NOTE: a leister

A trout to shallow-diving crankbait. (Photograph courtesy of Eric Weight)

is a spear or trident, usually used in conjunction with a light.]

Is it any more sportsmanlike to stand up to your thighs in water punching out a 10yd, high-density shooting head with a lure fly on the end than to flick out that same lure fly on – say – a 2oz spinning rod with a swan shot pinched on the line to aid casting? There are many situations where the latter presentation is likely to be more effective, less likely to spoil the pleasure of others and much more enjoyable to practise. And whichever way the trout happens to be killed, it's worth remembering that it's still a dead trout.

I've heard it said that if spinning was allowed, anglers who practised it would achieve their limits too quickly. So what? If that is their pleasure, and provided they do not fish on or return hooked fish so that they may continue to exploit a situation, what's wrong with that? It's unlikely to happen very often and it wouldn't make any difference anyway on a properly controlled fishery. If someone wants to get a limit and be off the water quickly, that's his

business. If he can seek to do it with a fly rod, why not with a spinning rod?

I've also heard it argued that, in any case, a good man with a fly rod will outcast and outfish a spinning enthusiast nine times out of ten. I think that is probably very true and all the more reason, in my book, for relaxing these method restrictions. The whole business is quite illogical. 'If we allow spinning we shall upset the fly fishers,' one fishery manager told me. But why? And what about the other anglers who are already upset about a situation which virtually bars them from fishing these public waters? Is it not possible to set aside certain areas for both methods? A short stretch of bank for light spinning, the remainder for fly fishing? And strictly to enforce the ruling that these areas are reserved for the methods nominated? That is important.

If I'm trying to cast and fish a nymph, I do not want someone beside me hurling out a spoon; but by the same token, if I'm delicately casting my tiny ½oz lures on my little spinning wand, I don't want someone beside me ripping the water open with a no. 10 shooting head.

The Thames Water Authority has already experimented with 'all-method' waters. It is hoped, after a suitable period, to be able to compare the effectiveness of different angling methods and then to decide upon policy, rules and regulations. A sensible attitude.

It has been suggested to me by those in control of certain fisheries that spinning areas would not be taken full advantage of and that this would result in less space for the fly fishers, but so far it has not been put to the test. If, after a given period, it was found that the spinning sections were not being exploited, there could be no argument; but I do not believe this would be the case. I do think, however, that a great many anglers using the spinning sectors would eventually take up fly fishing.

I think we might see a situation develop where a spinner, having all but taken his limit in the morning, might well spend the rest of the day with a fly rod. Alternatively, the fly fisher, having flogged away nearly all day for no reward, might feel justified in having the odd hour on the spinning sector in the hope of catching the brace of fish he's rashly promised his neighbour. I'm quite certain in my mind that the overall result of such administration would be an increase in the number of fly fishers and an increase in revenue for the public undertakings generally.

A few snobs might stay away in protest, but snobs are unlikely to be true sportsmen and they would probably not be missed. They've never tried spinning for trout, but they're prepared to condemn it out of hand. I have caught trout by all methods and many experiences have proved interesting. Henry's Lake in northern Idaho, for instance, holds large numbers of remarkably big trout. The fishing there is free. Facilities such as boat hire, cabin rental,

and so on, have to be paid for and a state licence is required before the water can be fished. The money from the state licence is used for conservation generally and it would seem that this fabulous water is very much self-supporting in the way of fish stocks. The rainbows and cutthroats hybridize and grow big; stocks take care of themselves.

Henry's Lake is referred to often by Americans as the 'fish factory' and yet there is absolutely no restriction on method. You may float fish with worms, bait cast with plugs or spoons, ledger with cheese, troll or trail with minnows and, if you like, you can buy salmon eggs for bait from the local store. It's quite the most exciting fishery I've ever visited. Spinning is widely practised, but it happens to be a fact that over

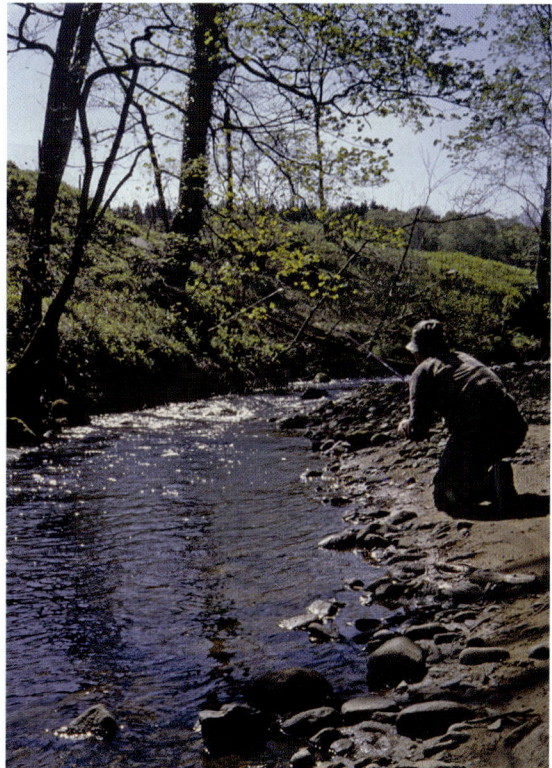

Barrie chasing wild brownies in North Yorkshire.

109

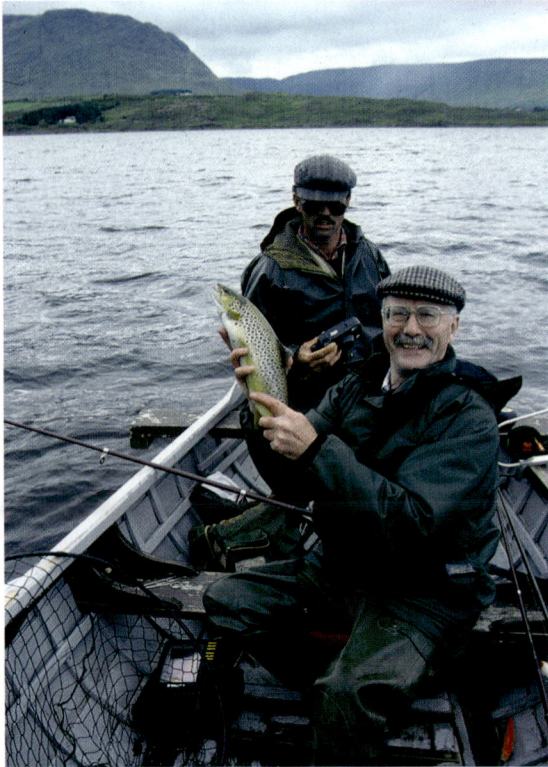

A nice brownie on Lough Mask, Ireland.

ninety per cent of the fish caught there are taken on fly. They are caught that way because for the most part it is the deadliest way of catching fish from that water. The spinners have been quick to learn this, but other methods are still permitted. I imagine it will always be so. There are times when the spinners have a ball, but any suggestion of 'slaughtering fish' is taken care of by the bag limit imposed.

There have been times when great slaughter has been brought about by fly fishers over here, but there has never been any suggestion of banning the fly. The petty rules and restrictions applied on reservoirs and public waters, where the object is supposedly to attract customers, give pleasure and derive income, have done much to maintain the great wall between coarse and game fishers that has existed throughout the last century. In fairness, however, it must also be said that the development of these public waters has done much to break down the barrier. By now it should have been flattened.

Is it not a pity that we cannot all fish as we would like? To enjoy experimenting with methods and presentations? To be able to put your thoughts and ideas into action without fear? To be discouraged from even 'bending' the rules? The list of forbidden methods increases and pretty soon we shall be unable to experiment at all. If that happens there will be no more pleasure left in the sport of fishing for me and hundreds like me. That's the part of it all that worries me.

Don't misunderstand me. I do not wish always to spin for trout, but I would like to feel I could do so when I felt so inclined. I would like that freedom because I happen to know that there are situations where it is warranted and where it could no harm whatsoever.

Thankfully, a few places remain where spinning is not a dirty word and, of course, if we forget those put-and-take waters, which provide an exciting but nevertheless somewhat artificial kind of fishing, and look further afield to the lochs of Scotland and the loughs of Ireland, there's a wealth of still-water spinning to be enjoyed. Strictly speaking, of course, lochs and loughs are not still waters, but for the purposes of distinguishing between them and rivers I will refer to them as such. And, although the fish in these wild waters are produced naturally and without the help of stew ponds and trout pellets, there are certain similarities in their behaviour. In very hot weather, for example, the big browns tend to lie deep and although I do not pretend to know why, there seems to be a certain magic about the 40ft-depth layer. Fred Buller, using char rigs and trailing fly-type lures at depths of

Barrie playing a good rainbow on a Yorkshire river. The fish was returned.

up to 70ft caught a number of big brown trout at the 40ft level.

Similar results have been achieved in other waters, both here and abroad, and it seems utterly ridiculous to me that I should be forced to fish for these deep-lying brown trout in our put-and-take reservoirs with traditional fly tackle. There is no possible way of getting a fly down to that depth and fishing it in a manner likely to attract trout. It could be done with spinning tackle from a boat and I see no reason why deep trolling with big spoons, plugs or spinners should not be allowed. These lures could be used with appropriate leads and, where necessary, in order to reach extreme depths, modern down-rigger equipment could be used. Deep trolling with down-riggers is not a particularly exciting way of fishing until the actual moment of contact. Then it becomes something else.

It works extremely well on the Irish loughs and I've no doubt it could be made to work very effectively in our deep English reservoirs. The diagram on page 75 shows roughly how it works. The plug, spoon, spinner or feathered lure is taken down in a quick release clip attached to a heavy paravane-shaped lead weighing several

pounds. This lead is attached to a wire line and is lowered by means of markings (or a sophisticated depth counter) to the appropriate depth. The lure works happily in its wake, but, being attached to an otherwise completely unfurnished rod and line, it breaks away from the release clip when a trout hits. The lead remains at the right depth, the fish is played to the surface on the light, limber spinning rod and the lure is sent down again on a new release clip with a free-sliding ring attachment. All very uncomplicated once the rigs have been set.

Speed of the boat is important and must be allied to the lure's action and the mood of the trout. Only experience can tell you when the boat is moving too quickly or too slowly. It takes time and patience, but is rewarding and there's more than a fair degree of skill involved. You have to be more of a boat handler than a rodsman, but it 'all comes good' with practice. It is, I venture to say, the only way of coming to terms with big deep-lying trout in any vast still water.

The dam-ends of many English reservoirs are so placed as to make fly casting impossible. The high wall behind allows no room for an extended back cast, the deep water immediately to the front cannot be exploited to the full with fly tackle. It is, however, an ideal spinning situation and where it is allowed there is no better method for exploring the depths. The techniques of spinning, rates of retrieve, how plugs and other lures work have already been explained in other chapters. There is no need for me to elaborate. I do not believe it's necessary to use huge lures (despite the fact that rainbows will take them) and I have long since come to the conclusion that a violent action on the part of the lure is often quite unnecessary. I have my own fancies, fads and favourites. I've used them in the wild waters of the Outer Hebrides, the Rocky Mountains, the Canadian wilderness, the Oregon desert, Ireland and in four of the American Great Lakes as well as our own English waters. I have caught, from these many places, brookies, browns, lakers, rainbows, cutthroats and hybrids – all on traditional spinning tackle used one way or another.

I do not make the above statement to prove what a clever angler I am, because, truthfully, I'm not so smart. But I do want to make it clear that spinning is an effective and sporting way of catching many kinds of trout in many different situations. For the record I prefer (and it is purely a personal preference) to use lure-type flies of one kind or another rather than bar spoons, plugs, Devon minnows, and so on. But because I have restricted myself voluntarily to lure-type flies made of hair, fur, tinsel, feather and the like, I've had to learn to dress them or arm them with sufficient weight to allow me to cast them with a spinning rod. There are many ways it can be done and possibly the simplest is to have already made-up a number of swan shots painted with black and white markings to resemble eyes. One of these can be pinched onto the line at the very point of attachment to the hook; it makes an ordinary streamer of bucktail

fly look even more like a small fish, plus it allows it to be cast on a light spinning outfit. Extra weight may be needed for longer-range casting and in my experience it is better to attach this in the form of extra swan shots pinched on immediately above and more or less touching the first. Up-trace leads will certainly add distance to the cast, but they give a strange feeling of being 'out of touch' during the retrieve. Somehow you're never quite sure just what the lure is doing when you've a chunk of lead between you and it. But with the lead bulked at the extreme end of the tackle (you may pinch shots onto the shank of the hook if there's room), there's a feeling of contact which is both agreeable and effective.

It doesn't take much imagination to dream up ways and means of making simple fly-type lures with weight built into them for casting purposes. There's no great skill involved (even I can make them), but they're fun to play around with; and they catch fish. All kinds of coloured embellishments may be added to any of the weighted hooks shown on pages 118–119 and I will not suggest any special dressings because they simply are not necessary. Any streamer fly dressing tied to one of these weighted hooks will catch fish on its day. Your problem is finding the right one for the day in question, but black, white, yellow and orange, or a combination of any two, are the colours I have found to be most effective.

Whichever way you choose to weight your hooks, use an Araldite-type glue generously in the process and let it set hard before adding the final dressings. Don't fuss about the dressing. It's easy to tie on a few more feathers or a wisp or two of hair when they've become worn. And remember too that very often these lure flies are most effective when they're well worn. They're often just 'coming good' when it's time to discard or re-dress them. The diagram on page 118 shows a fly vice being used to make up these lures, but you can work miracles with an ordinary pair of tweezers and a cotton reel. Slide the cotton reel up the tweezers and the jaws will close tightly enough to hold almost any size of hook.

All this has little to do with the actual casting and retrieving of lures with a spinning rod. It has little to do with the playing and landing of trout, but you have my word for it that the lures I'm describing here will work excellently with a lightweight spinning outfit and that they will catch fish. It's difficult to sit at a desk and tell someone how to fish, but I believe it is possible to pass on general information on what to use. These little snippets of information have been accumulated over many years of what I call open-minded angling. I do not believe they are common knowledge and I welcome the opportunity to pass them on, knowing that they have served me well in the past.

This is no place for a deep study of depth and temperature, but any observations in this particular field should be duly noted and allied to the speed, action, depth and colour of the lures being used. I cannot say: 'Do this when conditions are thus.' If I did, it wouldn't work. All I can say is: 'Take note, experiment and learn to put two and two together.' There are, of course, many other factors to consider when fishing deep, still waters for trout, but, again, observation is probably more important than technique. Finding fish, even without the restriction of the fly-only rule, is not always easy. Catching one fish does not necessarily mean others are present, but it's at least a possibility. If you have caught a trout from – say – a drifting boat by casting a lure, do you know at what depth the lure was working? After the fish has finally come to the net, do you know exactly where you hooked it? You'll have drifted some way since it happened; can you now go back to the same spot again? If you are trolling (or trailing)

a spinning lure behind a boat (allowed on some waters and certainly encouraged in many Irish loughs and Scottish lochs), are you certain you know the depth at which the lure is working? If you change it – will the second lure fish at the same depth, or deeper? Small points, but all-important regarding the whereabouts of fish.

The diagram on page 76 shows a simple marker for pinpointing a 'taking spot'. Immediately a trout is hooked, toss the marker over the side of the boat. Its oblong shape ensures that the weight will keep stripping off the line, turning the block over and over until the bottom is reached. Then it will stop and no more line will be pulled off. The 'buoy' will rest immediately above the lead and mark the spot with deadly accuracy.

Big Irish and Scottish waters will be easier to understand if a transistorized sonar unit is put to use. Depth is then accurately recorded, but a simple way to ascertain the actual depth at which a lure is fishing is to row deliberately over a known shallow area and judge from what happens there. You may be surprised to find that your lure is fishing not 18ft as you'd thought, but less than half that depth.

There's much more, of course. I could go on discussing still-water trout from now to eternity, but I'd be repeating some of the basics of spinning already dealt with in other chapters. I hope, however, that I've given you something to think about if and when the opportunity to spin for trout in still waters comes your way.

Rivers and Streams

The traditional way of spinning for trout in rivers is to tie on a small bar spoon with a violent, vibrating action, cast it upstream and retrieve it slightly faster than the current speed. These tiny bar spoons,

113

mostly of French, Swedish or Norwegian origin, work extremely well even when travelling with the current and they catch fish. Because they are armed with treble hooks, however, they tend to be hard on small trout; and in the event that it is necessary or deemed advisable to return an unwanted or undersized specimen, these three points of penetration often make the task impossible. It depends, of course, on what you want from your fishing. If, as I have done many times in wild and desolate areas, you are fishing for breakfast to be cooked over a camp fire, every fish, irrespective of size, will count – until sufficient have been caught. Then the fishing stops and the feeding begins. Half a dozen gudgeon-sized brownies taste just as good as one half-pounder when they're on the plate with an equal number of bacon rashers.

If, however, you're out to catch a brace or two of fish over a certain size and have no desire to hang onto the smaller ones, spinning with traditional treble-hooked spoons is not the answer. Some of the fly-type lures already described and also those shown in the diagrams on pages 118–119 will be equally effective and less harmful to any fish that is to be returned to the water alive. Another way round the problem is to snip off two points of the bar spoon treble and fish with only one. Odd fish will escape and almost certainly some of them will be of a takeable size, but at least they will be there for another time.

It is not always necessary to cast upstream to trout, however, and there are times when the action produced by retrieving against the current – that is, by casting downstream and retrieving upstream, will prove to be a better proposition. Remember one thing, however. Trout, like all other fish, spend much of their time headed into the current – which means that the downstream casting requires more caution on your part. You are more likely to be spotted

when you are stationed upstream of a fish, but good use of cover and common sense will usually take care of that problem.

There are many tiny, overgrown streams where the trout are small and plentiful, but which remain neglected by anglers either because their potential is not recognized, or because the nearby salmon or sea trout are considered more worthwhile. Personally, I like to fish such waters. I like to get into the stream, work my way slowly up, casting below the overhanging branches and flicking the tiny spoon or weighted fly into the likely looking spots. I like to force my way through the undergrowth and try some downstream casts through the areas I have not disturbed by wading and while I will use fly and worm with equal pleasure if I think it is advisable, I often find the former quite impossible and the latter sometimes too easy. Worm-caught fish are also, in my experience, usually dead fish. There's no stopping a hungry little brownie from committing suicide. In these waters, a half-pounder is a veritable monster and I'm never really sure about what to do with such fish. Should I return them because they are so few and far between? Or should I retain them because they've reached their peak anyway? I can't advise anyone with regard to this problem – because I don't know the answer myself. I doubt, however, if it makes much difference either way.

Many of the big salmon rivers of Scotland are fairly stiff with trout, but it's a safe bet that those in the pools have seen every conceivable type of lure before. The gentle glides, the wide shallows and some of the big, deep eddies hold trout in abundance, however, and they will often respond to sensible spinning with ultra-light gear. Again, the basics of spinning with ultra-light tackle have already been explained and there is little more to add.

The peaty burns of Scotland, the Welsh hill streams, the tiny becks of Cumberland all abound with small trout, and whether or not you regard the effort involved in catching them as a worthwhile occupation depends entirely upon your own temperament. I do. And again, I like to spin for these fish with weighted fly-type lures. The fish are easier to catch with baits such as small worms and maggots; but why struggle with what amounts to coarse fishing tackle when a tiny wand weighing a mere couple of ounces and a hatful of weighted flies will serve almost as well? Traditional fly fishing will catch these fish too, but again there are very few places where it can be practised.

I hesitate to mention Thames trout because they are a breed of fish in a class of their own; but they are not extinct yet and every once in a while, a weir pool in the upper reaches produces a big brownie to a spinner. I have taken the odd fish from the Kennet on spun minnows and while these might possibly be regarded as Thames trout, I do not consider myself knowledgeable enough to delve deeply into the subject. I believe, however, that some of the weir pools are worth exploiting occasionally during the coarse fish close season if only to learn just how difficult a problem is presented.

Referring briefly to the illustrated fly-spinners on pages 118–119, Fig. (a) is made from a long-shanked hook with a wire loop soldered on about one-third of the way along it. The whole is weighted with lead wire and almost any kind of feather or hair will do for dressing. The important point about this lure is that the line is attached to the wire loop and not the eye of the hook. This loop must he bent backwards or forwards until the lure is seen to be wobbling rapidly in the current. You need to see this effect before you can appreciate its deadliness. Retrieve upstream for best effect.

Fig. (c) shows a similar streamer fly with a wobbling disc (cut from an aluminium beer can) attached forward. Again, some bending and juggling is needed to get the required effect.

Fig. (d) shows a simple popping bug. Not normally associated with trout fishing at all, it has, on occasions, proved extremely effective for rainbows in deep, smooth runs during the so-called dog days of July. It is hardly a spinning-rod lure, but it can be cast downstream, allowed to float down even further and then retrieved with a series of 'pops'. Sometimes the effect is very dramatic. The same lure used at night sometimes produces similar results, but Fig. (b) shows an even better lure for that particular operation.

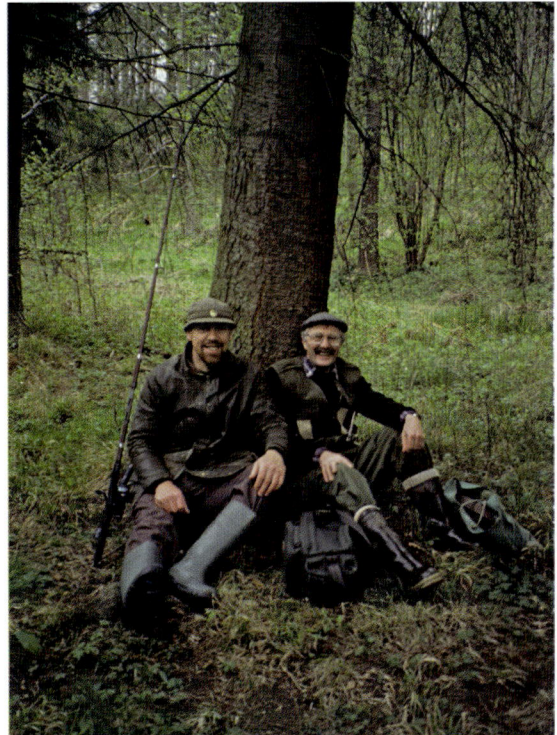

Barrie and Bill Winship after a morning's lure fishing for brownies. They had just enjoyed a good lunch of fried brownies, brown bread and butter.

13 Game Fishing: Sea Trout

The sea trout, sea-running *Salmo trutta,* has always been popular with game fishermen of both bait and fly persuasions. Perversely, as quality sea-trout fishing has become scarcer, hunting sea trout has become more popular and this is reflected in the recent publication of several outstanding books on the subject, such as James Waltham's *The Sea Trout and the Fly* (*see* Bibliography). I'll talk about some of Waltham's 'flies' later in this chapter.

For me, sea trout spinning, as well as fly fishing, began in the later 1950s when I regularly poached, with the farmer's connivance, a tributary of the famous River Lune. I learnt two things then, about time, which has never been contradicted by later experiences. One is that night is the best time for sea trout. The other is that there is a certain time in a waning flood when the colour is just right for spinning for sea trout. I'll say

A sea trout of 8lb plus from Abbey Mill fishery. (Photograph courtesy of Dave Steuart)

a little more about night fishing later in this chapter, but for the moment will concentrate on floodwater conditions.

When the river is bank-high and thickly brown, and visibility into the water is nil, that is the time for worms. My farmer friend was a worming fanatic and even when we knew exactly where the fish were, I could catch little on lures when the water was so thick, whereas he pulled out fish after fish on worms. The reasons were obvious, because each dispatch prior to cooking revealed a mouth full of worms and slugs. But as the water cleared and the level dropped lures became more effective than worms. As the water became clearer still, so that you could just see the bottom in a couple of feet of water, then lures fished deeper were more effective than lures fished near the top. I managed to persuade my farmer to try my lure rod and he promptly caught a 7lb fish, far bigger than anything I'd had on lures. Mine were usually up to 1¼lb or so.

When the water is really clear then spinning does become much more difficult and the sea trout man turns to fly as a rule. However, you *can* catch at this time, using some of the methods described by Dave Steuart in Chapter 11. Find the deeper water, the head of a pool, the rocky overhang, and hold the spinner down there on a paternoster rig. Or allow the paternoster rig to swing slowly across the deeper part of the pool. Or you can night-fish.

My night fishing has been done on rocky rivers and when I first started doing it, I fished shallow because I didn't want to lose my spinner in the boulders. It turns out that this is, generally, the thing to do. Fish the spinner in the surface layers or by actually dragging and sputtering across the surface.

Now let's go back to James Waltham's flies. Some of these are arguably flies, although I prefer to call some of them small plugs. His Cockroach surface lure may have a little hackle, but it's a plug. So is his head-eyed Jimbo and his popper-headed Snake Fly. Other anglers have done the same with their flies, namely put on something like a diving vane which turns them, in my book, into a plug or a non-fly lure: you can see some illustrations in this chapter. I don't have any moral problem with any of this. It simply puts them well into the context of this book. I haven't had the nerve to try these surface-dragged lures during the day, but I wonder if it would work – in coloured water perhaps? I only raise the question because I *have* used fast-dragged dry flies on the Irish loughs, taking nice brown trout, though as yet no sea trout.

The questions of *when* to fish the spinner in coloured water in daytime, and what lures to use at night, probably varies greatly with the water in question. Certainly the perfect colour differs from water to water and in real spate waters the window of opportunity may only be open for thirty minutes or so. I have noticed that on the spate streams on which I have spun, those that are less overshadowed by trees produced fish earlier in the fining-down period. This was so obvious at times that I'd deliberately move into the overhung stretches as the water colour dissipated. This does suggest visibility is the key factor.

Another factor is the spin pattern produced by different lures. In our book (*Spinning and Plug Fishing*), Ken Whitehead and I did flume tank experiments to see which lures flashed more strongly and in which patterns. Bar spoons emit a rhythmic and strong flash and one which repeats quickly. Spoons usually emit a lower flash, more slowly and less rhythmically. And that is my experience with sea trout: use bar spoons early, when the water is just approaching its optimum 'lure colour' and spoons as the water clears. This is only a rough guide, because I know waters where small plugs do better than either bar spoons or spoons, plus one water where all they will look at, at *any* stage of the colour, is minnows, quill minnows and the like. One of my best lures has been a small Toby-like slim spoon, but lacking the little fins of a Toby and having rather more of a concavo-convex curvature along its length; it wobbles more than the traditional Toby. One about 2–3in long is best. The problem is that I rarely see these for sale (the last time was in Australia, where I had large numbers of cocky salmon on them). At the moment I have none at all. Many experts add extra trebles to their lures, such as a small treble at the head of the Toby, or a trailing treble in the case of James Waltham's lures. I've always avoided this as much as possible, perhaps to my cost. In terms of colours, I suppose most of my fish came to blue and silver, a good number on the wobbler 'Toby', which is usually green and silver, and others with yellow in the colour. I don't have strong views on the subject.

Night fishing by whatever method is a very exciting way of taking sea trout, but on many waters great care needs to be taken. It goes without saying that a good daytime knowledge of the water is a help. Whilst many anglers frown at the use of a torch, I'd unhesitatingly use one if I was in doubt, especially when leaving a water. A tiny, dull torch can be used for changing lures. At night, I prefer a backpack to a shoulder bag, or I simply stuff things in my pocket. A rod and a landing net are enough to handle. The landing net handle should be sturdy enough to use as a staff

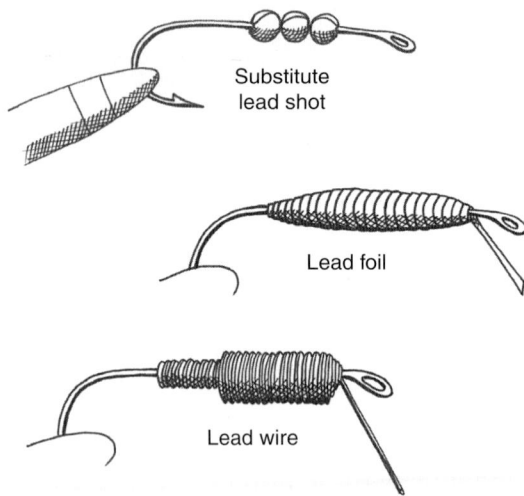

Initial stages of preparing leaded fly/lure for trout fishing: finished product below. The amount and type of weighting can be carried easily.

if necessary. The take of a sea trout in the dark is something never forgotten and with lures, at least, the takes are rarely missed, except some of those slashing takes at surface lures.

So far, I may have given the impression that mountain streams are the places to go,

but that is simply because my early experiences were on such waters. There are good sea trout fisheries on some of the big Irish loughs, for example, plus some of the big rivers, such as East Anglia's Great Ouse, have a run of big sea trout. Friends have had double-figure sea trout from the Great Ouse and the River Wissey, whilst the River Lark and River Little Ouse also have a sea trout run, as does the River Delph. One friend specializes in taking sea trout of 2–3lb from a distributary of the middle Great Ouse. Nobody seems to know of this water, but I have been there myself and done quite well. On the bigger rivers in the Fenlands the best lures seem to be salmon lures like the yellow-belly, or big blue and silver metal minnows. The retrieve needs to be seriously fast and usually not far below the surface. Finding the fish is difficult, but a dawn start, watching for leaps, is essential.

A lot of sea trout buffs specialize in that most challenging area of them all, namely the estuaries. Sea trout work the edges, hunting small fish and crabs. Some fully marine bays are also good sea trout places at times. The problem with these places is knowing *where* and *when*. The local

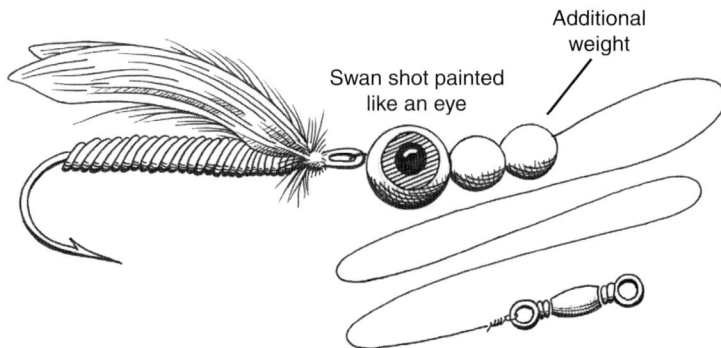

Leaded fly/lure.

A series of lures suitable for trout, sea trout, as well as other species: a) to be fished deep, as a jig, or shallower if attached to the first eye; b) surface lure with small propeller; c) lure with diving vane, in effect a tiny plug; d) surface popper, easy to make in foam or balsa.

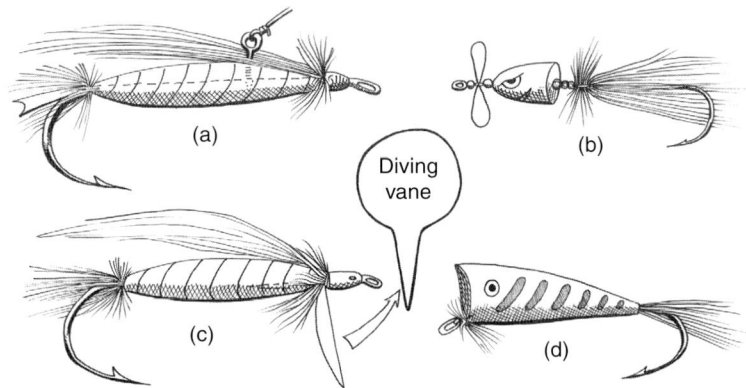

(a)

(b)

Diving vane

(c)

(d)

commercial fishermen will know (even if they pretend they are bass fishing; I was once shown a beach-to-buoy net, just drawn in, which the fishermen claimed was full of 4lb-ish 'bass'). Find those places and spin the shores, and you could be in with a chance at the right time of the year. I know another bay, in Yorkshire, where the mackerel and sea trout (but not bass) herd big shoals of fry into a gully. You catch far more mackerel than sea trout, but the latter are around 4lb; on hot August days, they are there, but the next day could be gone. I also know a place near a river mouth where a professional fisherman completely blocks the river with his net, which is illegal of course, and takes huge bags of sea trout, often in the 3–7lb bracket. I've tried this section many times with the 'right' lures, but so far have failed. I'll be back though. Such is the draw of lure fishing for sea trout.

14 Big Game Fishing

By David Bird

Having spent nearly twenty years or so fishing in sunnier climes, to get away from our long, depressing, damp winters, I've picked up a few tips and plenty of good advice on how to make sure the trip of a lifetime doesn't turn into a disaster.

Some years ago my wife Maggi and I won a holiday at some exotic hotel on the Mediterranean. A stream of faxes were soon winging their way to the hotel manager – what kind of fish, type of tackle available, model and age of boats, cost, and so on. I didn't get a reply. So, we never went. Not so long ago a South Coast charter skipper went on a safari holiday to East Africa and having a free day decided he might try his hand at big game fishing. Wandering down the beach he booked in with the first agency he saw. The result – a dirty old scow with poor-quality tackle and the crew smoking over open cans of petrol. I seem to remember he didn't even get a bite. Not the trip of a lifetime for him.

We all have biteless days, but if the skipper and crew are seen to be working hard and professionally on your behalf, the tackle may be old but is well maintained, the boat may also be old but is clean, tidy, reliable and doesn't belch black smoke to the horizon, then it lessens the disappointment considerably.

But you will still need to do a bit of homework, particularly if your partner and kids are in tow. If your beloved is happy with the accommodation and entertainment you're halfway there. Go onto the Internet and have a good look. Pick out a few packages of interest and send an e-mail or fax to the hotels and guest houses asking the relevant questions. Get in touch with the specialist holiday/fishing agencies covering your interest. Ask the pertinent questions. If you're unhappy with the responses – don't go.

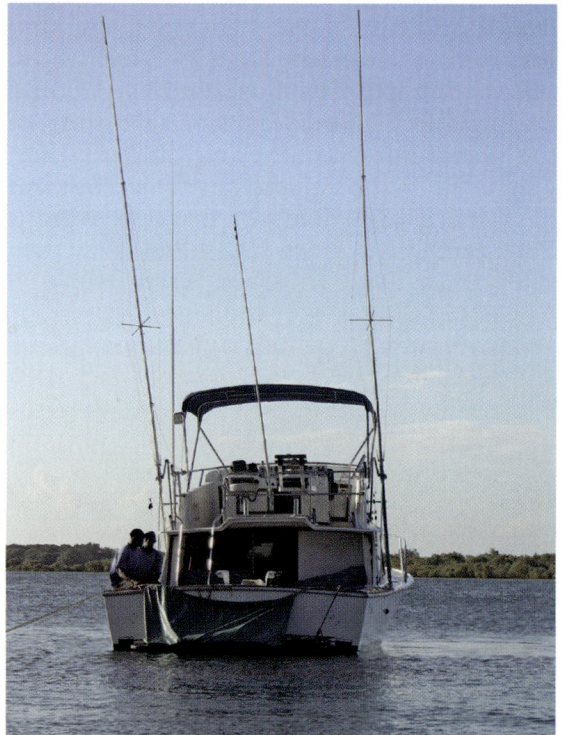

Big game fishing luxury craft, all ready to go.

How to Get There

For first timers, I would suggest going for the all-inclusive, door-to-door package, which may also include a personal guide who will help you to avoid the normal tourist pitfalls. Flights only, to exotic climes, can be difficult and here I can only offer you one choice – go to Dial-A-Flight. Not the cheapest, but the most professional. Fly-only deals are one area where it can go seriously wrong. Sitting for hours/ days in some third-world airport awaiting a connecting flight is low on the scale of enjoyment. A friend of mine won a holiday to fish for marlin in Costa Rica. Despite numerous calls to various airlines, he was getting nowhere fast. One call to Dial-A-Flight and within twenty-four hours a complete itinerary was flagged up on his e-mail address. Peace of mind is paramount, particularly if the family or friends are with you. In 'Useful Addresses' at the end of this book you will find details of some specialist fishing travel companies that I know and trust.

Precautions

Whatever country you're travelling to, check with the airline or travel agency as to what diseases, if any, you will need to be vaccinated against. Please take this seriously, especially if visiting third-world countries. Be aware that there is no jab available for malaria, which can be life-threatening. There are various courses of tablets that can be taken to stave off the infection, but I would recommend Malarone as the most effective at this time. You will need a prescription from your doctor and will need to pay for the course of treatment (£60/70 for three weeks cover in 2008). The good thing about the product is its simplicity. A pill a day, two days before you leave, during the

Big game lure, a bait fish plus its header attachment. (Photograph courtesy of David Bird and Total Sea Fishing)

holiday and three or four days after you get back. An easily remembered habit.

Why not keep the mosquitoes away in the first place? One of the least kept secrets is Avon Skin So Soft Soft and Fresh, dry oil spray. It really does work. *Spray exposed skin areas before you get off the plane. Spray exposed areas daily, particularly at evening time when the mossies are at their worst.* It's good for midges at home as well. Don't worry you macho types, the smell is quite pleasant without going over the top.

What to Take

With the current threats from global terrorism, airlines and airports are imposing stringent checks and procedures on all travellers. Please take the conditions seriously and conform to the letter. Abuse or make a joke of the situation and the security system will make sure you lose. In addition, the delays you cause will irritate other tourists.

It is better to have one piece of main hold luggage, within the weight limit, than two lighter ones, which are easier to pinch wherever you go. Don't make it easier for the criminal element. In addition, I place a generous wrapping of cling film around the areas of padlocks and closure devices. This performs two functions: it stops you and the baggage handler getting lacerated by the sharp edges of the padlocks and is a further deterrent to the thief who might nick a few items by levering up a corner of your suitcase.

When it comes to tackle it's a different ball game. No longer are small travel rod tubes allowed as a separate item of hand luggage in the overhead locker. Your minuscule tube might contain an air to-air missile, so into the hold it will go. If it doesn't fit in your suitcase I would suggest take it. On the brighter side, over recent years, a whole range of four-, five- and six-piece travel rods have come onto the market that will fit into a standard travel bag or case.

While it's nice to use your own kit, be mindful that the new species you are targeting, pound for pound, scrap a lot harder and are found in deeper water. You may land a 30/40lb carp on 12lb class kit at home, but a 15kg yellowfin tuna, giant trevally or amberjack in 300ft is a totally different proposition. As a guideline, if you want to take your own rod and reel, err on the heavier side, 20lb class minimum, although bordering on 30lb is better. Take a spare loaded spool – in sunnier climes fish can really spool you with ease. Try to supplement the tackle that's already available.

Here I would confess that I don't use multiple-section travel rods and try to squeeze them into my already stuffed luggage. I use standard one- and two-piece rods in a jumbo Bazooka tube. Remember what I said earlier – big, heavier or bold is best. But then again I'm prepared to pay for excess baggage or get an air ticket that gives me a generous weight allowance. The big tube works best if you are travelling in a group with all the rods in one gigantic equivalent of a drain pipe. However, you must all arrive at the check-in desk at the same time with your 'team leader', clearly stating that angling's weight equivalent to the Channel Tunnel is a shared baggage allowance.

Here's a little tip. Take a lightweight nylon, unlined waterproof jacket (weighs a couple of ounces and packs up small). You can get very wet if seas are choppy and it can rain in the sunniest climes. It also keeps the wind off if it gets a bit chilly, as it can do as the evenings draw on.

Protection

As you are aware, the advice and hints I am trying to pass on are geared to fishing in the 'hot zone' – the nearer to the equator you fish, the hotter it gets, of course. If you want to fish in Alaska or Iceland, get a hot water bottle or an electric blanket. Back to the sunshine. I have seen too many fishing holidays turned into a disaster, within a few days, because one or both of the partners has been confined to bed suffering from heatstroke or severe sunburn. Now is not the time for a macho bronzing stance whether you are dark skinned or fair.

Let me assure you that you will get the required tan, you so desire, very easily even if you follow my apparent draconian regime. I use Riemann P20 Once-a-Day Sunfilter; also recommended is Ultrasun High All Day Protection 20. It is important to remember that either product must have

A sequence showing the capture (and eventual return) of a giant of the seas. (Photograph courtesy of David Bird and Total Sea Fishing)

thoroughly dried before you venture out. Here's a chance to let your imagination run wild. On fishing days I get up fifteen minutes earlier than need be, have a quick shower, dry off thoroughly and apply a full coating of P20. Nude, I stand in front of the air-con outlet to speed up the drying process. My wife Maggi is underwhelmed by my posing.

Make sure your skin is dry before applying any lotion. Keep an eye on each other. When fishing with friends, we let each other know if it looks like one of us is burning. If fishing alone, my crew is given the same instruction. When at sea or on the 'flats', take extra care – the sun's reflection off the surface multiplies its effect. If in doubt, add another coat of sun protection, but don't just slap it onto the legs exposed by the shorts line or arms up to the sleeve level.

During the course of the day shirt sleeves and shorts can rise up without you realizing it. Pull the legs of your shorts and shirt sleeves up as far as they will go before applying the grease, but preferably slap it on before you get dressed. There are vulnerable body areas that are prone to serious sun damage – ear tips, lips and cheeks, so

make sure they're well-coated – Ultrasun Face 30 comes highly recommended. The same conditions as P20 apply – be dry when you apply. To preserve your tan and well-being it is important that you nightly apply a liberal coating of 'after-sun moisturizing cream'. This not a vanity thing, but is to stop you looking like a dried-up old prune and will prevent your fabulous tan peeling off. It will also make you feel more comfortable.

Clothing is certainly also an area worth investigation and investment for a comfortable, safer fishing holiday. This is not the time to be a fashion freak. 'Functional rather than pretty' is my motto. Loose-fitting, quick-drying clothing is the order of the day – there is a wide range of inexpensive microlight clothing available from specialist stores. If you burn easily, go for full-length trousers and long-sleeve shirts. I prefer shirts with collars, compared to tee shirts, for the extra neck protection. Next, get a decent cap or hat, giving maximum coverage with a wide peak or brim – not only to protect the head, but also to cut down on glare.

Take a spray can of dry iodine. Cuts, nicks and more serious wounds can go septic

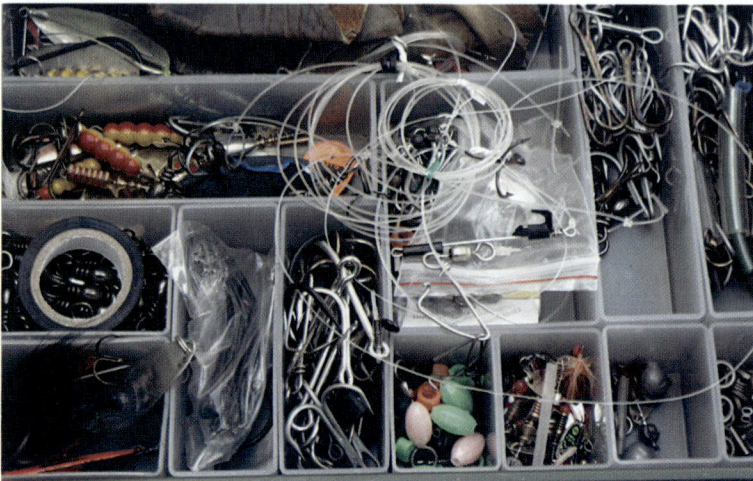

A big game kit box looks a bit different from the usual lure rig box.

Barrie out of control here. The Nile perch is on a long run and he's failing to keep the rod bent!

in the blink of an eye. I know it stings, but be brave.

Finally, sunglasses, or should I say fishing glasses? Most inexpensive or fashionable sunglasses aren't polarized and may make matters even worse for your eyes than none at all. They simply darken the view, causing the pupils to open and exposing them to even more harmful rays. Only polarized sunglasses protect against glare. Here again, I would suggest that you go against the current fashion and get full-size frames with side panels. The more glare you keep out, the more fish and wildlife you'll see. With the right glasses you will reduce eye strain. Costa Del Mar and Ocean Waves come highly recommended, but remember to get the right colour of lens to suit your style of fishing – grey for the bonefish flats and amber for deep blue water. Either will be advantageous for UK fishing: a bit on the expensive side, but well worth the investment. Add a retention band to secure the glasses in place so that you don't lose them overboard and you're ready to go.

Finally, a little tip. When it's nice, hot and sunny, boat anglers may be tempted to go barefoot. Please don't. I've seen too many accidents and near misses when big hooks,

particularly awesome trebles, are floating around the boat. Deck shoes are the order of the day (the canvas versions are pretty cheap and will give good service) – they're designed for the job and will give better grip when it's wet. The all-plastic Croc shoes will also fit the bill, but remember to put some sun protection on your feet as the sun will burn through the slots. Footwear is a must when fishing the flats for bonefish, because you'll never know what you will tread on.

The Tackle

Big game fishing and the range of tackle used can cover everything from big kona-type lures chasing grander black marlin to spinning small jigs and pirks for a variety of tunas. The rapala-type lure catching Nile perch on Lake Nasser will also catch king mackerel and wahoo in deep blue water off the Kenyan coast. At the right time of the year, a small plastic shrimp mounted on a size 8/0 circle hook will catch yellow-fin tuna – 80kg plus. A leaded bulb squid will catch a variety of fish on the drop. A range of pirks catching cod and pollock in the English Channel will also catch amber-jack and giant trevally anywhere down to 500–600ft in warmer waters. You will have to err on the heavier side and use braided line if you want to hit bottom in a reasonable time.

Likewise, rods, reels and lines will need to fit the targeted species. The secret to all big game fishing is balanced tackle. Whether it's 130lb class or 10lb, make the effort to get it right. When it comes to reels, multiplier or spinning, step up a size to what you would ordinarily use for a particular line strength. This will give the additional capacity often needed with long, deep-running fish. You can also lose a bit of line with no curtailment of your fishing. If you are a first-timer, seek professional advice from the specialist companies offering the trip of a lifetime. Nowadays, all tackle is laid on and the quality is pretty good.

Big game do things to the tackle!

A few years ago, fishing out of Hemingways Resort in Kenya and having caught a whole bunch of big fish, plus having pioneered giant trevally on 12oz and 16oz pirks (pink or blue are best), I heard that some big amberjack were turning up in mixed bags. I had it on good authority that these 'jacks gave a good account of themselves, so set out to target the species on my next two or three trips out to the East African coast. I needed some specialized tackle and a specialized single-minded approach. My regular skipper, Robbie Hellier, originally on the good ship *Ol Jogi*, would have to be retrained and taught to ignore the marlin and sailfish whose siren calls are from the rips, canyons and mountains – deep-water marks a few miles off the coast. He would have to pay more attention to what showed up on the echo sounder. Were the fish on the bottom, or 80 or 180ft off? What were they? Drop down a big pink or blue pirk and find out.

My quest to catch a big 'jack is what follows next. It is a good example of how big game fishing works: it puts all the foregoing theory into practice.

Amberjacked

When I was planning my annual September trip down Kenya way, chasing big yellowfin tuna, I decided to follow up the rumour of a recently landed 80kg amberjack. This is world-beating stuff, with the current record around the 70kg mark. A little bit of investigation soon found out that a big amberjack had been boated, but was only in the 60kg range – accidentally caught while bottom fishing. Still, a stunning fish and very much worth pursuing. This fish's reputation for long, protracted, down deep and dirty fighting tactics had me drooling to have a go. I should backtrack here a little to put you in the picture.

I started fishing out of Hemingways Resort in Kenya in 1994, general stuff, trolling for sailfish and other surface-feeding game fish. It was during these activities that the fish finder kept showing big bunches of fish hugging the bottom and down the sides of the various reefs and banks. Skipper Pete Glover and I decided that we ought to try to see what they were and if they were worth catching. A couple of years later, armed with an assorted range of big pirks, we dropped down onto the fish. The first take was a surprise – a 25kg wahoo caught on the drop. We caught a lot of giant trevallys, one of my favourite fish. In the meantime, Pete had moved on to farm up country and I palled up with Robbie Hellier on *Ol Jogi*.

We persevered and were soon into a whole range of trevallys, golden, blue and big-eye with some red snapper thrown in for good measure. Some of the trevallys could have been in line for the record books if we hadn't been following tag and release. The best day was twenty huge giant trevallys over 20kg, with the biggest nudging 45kg. We lost count of the smaller fish. All were tagged and released. As the pirking caught on, new marks and a wider range of fish were found. In recent years this included the odd amberjack, until last year when one of the boats connected with ten of these beasties, best around 35kg on a 500ft deep-water mark normally only bottom-fished for red snapper for the hotel table.

A bit of homework was needed before tackling hard-fighting fish in deep water. Obviously, we needed to switch to braid to reduce the effect of the strong currents and 500ft of water between fish and boat.

Experience also showed that fast-retrieve reels were essential for the right presentation to maximize the bite-to-drop ratio. I'd recently been looking at the SR-30 Twin Spin, the new big spinning reel from Accurate. With its twin drag giving up to 40lb pressure, 6:1 retrieve rate and the capacity for 600m of 60lb braid, it looked like the perfect tool for the job. A Rolls-Royce price, but worth the investment. A quick call to Russell Weston at Snowbee soon had one on my doorstep ready to be spooled up.

Next, what rod? Past experience had shown that an 8ft tool with a softish tip to absorb the initial take with plenty of guts in the middle section should fit the bill. Ben Sturt at Wildfly put together the ideal package – 30/60lb Pac Bay blank, heavy duty line guides with a solid aluminium butt with gimbal and a long foregrip for maximum leverage. He added a specially designed clip above the reel seat so that I could harness up in the event of a hard, long slog to get the fish on board. This clip also doubles as the best point to attach a

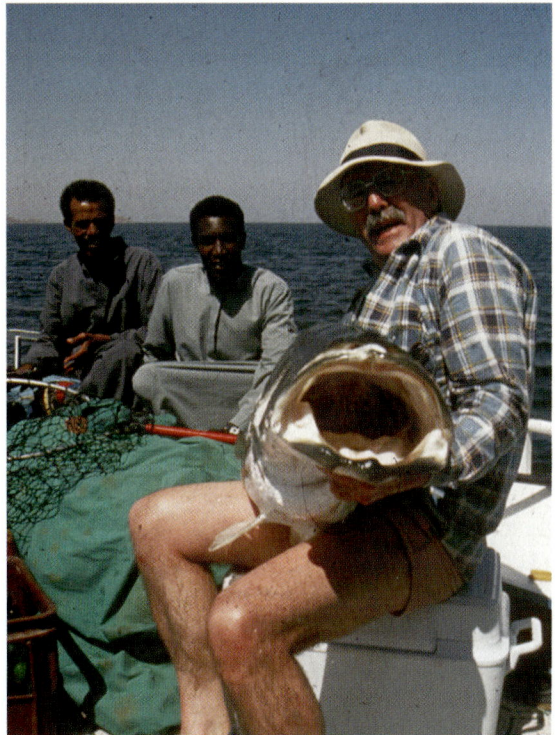

Why some fish will take big lures.

127

The worst moment in lure fishing, a head-shaker which throws the lure clear (see lure, top left).

safety line – instead of clipping the line to the bale arm or reel handle – removing potential damage to the reel.

I then put together a collection of pirks of varying hues from 10–16oz and was ready to go. With my normal enthusiasm that a record might be on the cards I checked with the International Game Fishing Association (IGFA) to see if the butterfly hook rigs were legal. The two hooks with same size links were not acceptable. To comply with the IGFA ruling the links needed to be of different lengths so that the eye of the bottom hook was below the bend of the top hook. A selection of rigs was put together to cope, I hoped, with every eventuality.

The weather in Kenya during September can be a bit hit and miss as the seasons change. Rough seas (Force 6 to 7) with a liberal dash of rain is normal until the wind settles from the north. Robbie was anxious to christen his new boat, *Un-Reel*. We had a few practice runs out of Watamu on well-known marks – rips, canyons and mountains – catching good bags of yellowfin up to the 25kg mark before dropping down 10oz pirks to where we hoped the amber-

jack might be hiding. Two savage takes resulted in popped lines under the pressure of the fish and the five-knot tide. We needed to tighten into the fish a lot quicker. We pressed on for the next two days without another take.

A change of tactics saw us move the boat 40 miles up the coast to the saltwater creek at Ngomeni, ready to attack the North Kenya Banks over the next three fishing days I'd booked. The programme was to leave the hotel at 4.45am, drive up to Ngomeni and then two hours at top speed to the banks.

During those three days the fishing was unbelievable: we were surrounded by yellowfin tuna in the 5–25kg range that took the lures at every depth – surface down to 500ft. An estimated one ton of fish came to the boat. The big 50kg+ fish didn't show, although we thought we saw the odd one breach in the distance. But never mind, we were now after amberjack.

Our pirks winged their way to the bottom. Yellowfin and red snapper bit whatever we did. And then, a scorching run. My first 'jack was on. Twenty minutes of hard graft before it came to the boat. Its weight? A measly 12kg. Heaven knows what it's like to get a really big one! Then my fishing partner, Phil Revett, hooked his first amberjack. Half an hour of frenetic tug of war and it was his. Puffing and panting, he couldn't believe it weighed just 14kg. Phil then latched onto our biggest 'jack at around 17kg. Forty minutes later we were looking at one awesome fish that took no notice of our beefed-up pirking gear. Then, not another take.

Phil was of the opinion that there were just too many yellowfin getting in the way. As match men say when plagued by small fish – we were 'bitted out' by too many tuna. But, we were total amberjack converts.

Rematch

Packing my fishing kit ready for my jaunt down Kenya way in mid-January I got to thinking what effect some 20-odd kilos of heavy lead pirks, ready wired rigs and soft lures might have when passing through the airport security system. Big flashing red lights and wailing sirens? 'It's OK, just a loony fisherman moving a tackle shop out of the country.' And what about my jumbo rod tube? Needless to say, Maggi and I passed through Gatwick without a hitch in spite of the increased security.

Back to Hemingways Resort for another crack at the giant amberjack just waiting to take one of my lures. Robbie Hellier, skipper of the good ship *Un-Reel*, had been plotting some interesting marks where I might hook up on my dream fish. In my modesty, a 30–40kg amberjack would have been more than satisfying, but Robbie's 60kg monster was still haunting me. When arriving in Kenya I usually take the first couple of days to sort out my tackle, respooling reels, checking and assembling

David Bird with a giant Amberjack, taken in Kenya, 2008.

rigs and traces, as well as catching up on the gossip at the bar. One or two of the other skippers had landed a few fish nudging the target weight so my optimism was running high. There were quite a few big sailfish and black, blue and striped marlin being taken out at 'The Rips' on lures and live-baited frigate mackerel (friggies). But they could wait for another day.

On the first foray I was joined once again by Phil Revett who was also anxious to nail a big 'jack. Back to 'The Mountains', a big-water reef some 12 miles out where we caught and lost a few in September the year before. After three hours of hard manual labour pirking in 450ft of water we only had three small amberjack around the 10kg mark to the boat plus a smattering of red snappers. Other patches were investigated but no fish were showing on the sounder. Not a good start. We spent the rest of the day consoling ourselves by trolling a range of small lures to catch a nice mix of wahoo, yellowfin tuna and rainbow runners which gave good sport on light line.

On day two I was joined by Ben Thomas from Bishop's Stortford who was on his first big game trip. He was happy to catch anything on the big side, but was especially keen to catch the 'jacks I'd been incessantly burbling on about. Second drop and Ben latched into a 12kg fish which gave him a good workout. Then I was in. Some twenty minutes later Robbie shouted down, 'You've got your biggie, go for it.' Some fifteen more agonizing minutes and up popped a foul-hooked 15kg fish. No wonder it was hard work. Disappointed? Just a tad.

We soldiered on and boated a few more around the same stamp before trolling the long way home with the usual mixed bag. The amberjack were proving difficult to nail down. Some of the bunches of fish showing on the bottom were 70ft high, but numerous drops couldn't buy a bite. Other times the take was on the first lift. Then the 'jacks would strike at the top of the bunch. We would get two or three takes, then nothing. Frustrating doesn't cover it.

I then had an enforced five-day lay off because all the boats had been previously booked for a South African Billfish Competition. Time for a rethink. One of the skippers commented that when bottom-fishing with six hooks baited with fish strip for snapper he often had the snappers taken by amberjack and landed the odd fish which seemed to be on the bigger side. A plan at last. Start the day bottom-fishing with a pirk dropped down either side and wait for the struggling snapper to entice the amberjack into the catching zone. Couldn't be simpler.

It was also now getting to the stage where the sailfish and marlin on the Rips couldn't be ignored and Robbie was getting anxious to get a few tag-and-release flags on his outrigger. So the plan was to spend the first three hours following the master plan, then make a speedy run out for the billfish. I was joined by Stuart Fitzgibbon and Linda Heath from Dorking and the day started well with Stuart bringing aboard his first 'jack after a hard fight that left him exhausted. A couple more were boated, along with a strange mix of snappers which I'm still trying to identify. Pirking in 450ft is just hard slog, so a quick bite of early lunch and then onwards for Stuart and Linda's first sailfish on friggie live baits.

With two more days to go I was joined by old Kenya hand Alan Sibley, who wanted to try lighter tactics for the 'jacks. His speciality ended up with a series of sizable snappers which neither of us recognized. I think the 'jacks were on holiday. Hard graft for small reward. That's fishing for you.

My final day arrived; follow the master plan with Phil Revett back on board, having just returned from an animal safari, on the Masai Mara just west of Nairobi.

Robbie came up with a little twist we should try. Put down a friggie deadbait on the bottom fishing rig – what's to lose? Time was running out for my specimen amberjack. Dropping a deadbait down 450ft did create a few problems with line twist and the trace spinning round the reel line. Patience was needed to slow down the descent and present the bait. When we got it right – a bite. The first two or three were missed because of the crew's enthusiasm to strike at every little twitch of the rod tip. 'Give 'em time,' shouted Robbie.

Orders obeyed. Hook up. On an 80lb class kit the 20kg fish gave a good account of itself, even with a 4lb lead weight banging on its nose. Then ... whack. I was in. Some forty minutes later my first 20kg+ plus fish came to the gaff. They're delicious, by the way. Hard work, so a quick cold drink, a bacon sarnie, a leisurely smoke and back down again. Some 80ft off the bottom it hit. The fish was spooling me; tighten the drag and hang on. The third run slowed and I gained a few yards of precious line. Then promptly lost it. Time and again this awesome fish punished me as no other.

Then the line went tight and dead.

'It's gone into a hole in the reef,' shouted a very frustrated Robbie. 'Slacken off to see if it will come out.' No sooner said than done – to no avail. The line parted. Forty minutes of pure angling pleasure and adrenaline rush. I did end the day with a 22kg fish, which softened my disappointment.

The final session finished with two sailfish and two striped marlin, tagged and released. Robbie got his flags. Over a few cold drinks on the veranda, Robbie mentioned that he had a photo of the 60kg monster 'jack on his computer – would I like to see it? Certainly would! The computer fired up, but no photo; it was lost in the ether somewhere. A swift e-mail to the captor resulted in a copy shortly after I got home. It's a monster. I'll be back. Lesson learned: I had been using a black spirit marker pen to darken the first 10ft of the brightly coloured braid to the trace so as not to frighten the fish. Don't do it. Three lost fish on the trot showed that the spirit had severely weakened the line.

Editor's Note

David Bird's chapter is an edited version of several articles originally published by *Total Sea Fishing* magazine, and we gratefully record our thanks for permission to use the material here in book form.

15 Sea Fishing

Sea fishing with lures could be regarded as the grandaddy of the sport: sea anglers have always been tuned in to lure fishing, much more so than their freshwater counterparts. Just think, now, how backward was lure fishing for pike or game fish in the 1950s. It's only in the new millennium that those sports have come of age. Yet sea anglers have been at it all along and doing fine, whether using mackerel spinners for mackerel, plugs for bass, pirks for cod, or megalures for big game. Big game was dealt with in Chapter 14 by David Bird, so here I will discuss sea spinning as though you were a coarse/pike angler thinking of taking up sea spinning. This is a good way of approaching the matter, partly because of what has gone before in the book, but also because it will help you to avoid some of the pitfalls.

The first thing we have to face is that most sea fish fight a lot harder on the same tackle than do freshwater fish. I began sea spinning at the same time as I took up sea fishing in general, in the 1950s, in Yorkshire. Of course, I'd 'done' mackerel on spinner both from boats out of Scarborough and Bridlington and from piers and sea fronts. Other fish were caught too, such as small coalfish. But you get a much better fight out of a 1lb mackerel than you do from a 5lb pike or a 3lb trout, so the idea of just using coarse tackle needs a bit of caution. I've used a MK IV carp rod for catching codling and, to be frank, I wouldn't do it again.

Pollack sculpture.

132

A 3lb+ wrasse taken by Barrie in Tasmania on a reflector spoon from a deep, turbulent gully full of seaweed.

It's best to get the right rods and reels for the much more robust sport of sea fishing. Pike and salmon spinning rods are fine for some sea spinning, as long as they do not have a through action. Once you get on a boat and may be using big leads to get the lure down to the fish – be it a pirk for a cod or a rubber sand eel for bass and pollack – then the rod will need to be beefed up to 20lb class, 30lb class, or whatever the boatmen or local experience dictates. The reels can be big fixed spool reels or multipliers – sea anglers seem to use both,

although I still think far too few of them use left-hand-wind multipliers when they are right-handed.

Sea anglers always surprise me by using lighter lines than I would be inclined to use, so, if you'll excuse my way of putting it, the ex-coarse angler should not, in this regard anyway, feel too much at sea. For lure fishing at sea you'll be using lines from around 6lb bs up to 60lb bs in both monofil and braid. If you are taking up sea spinning it's a good idea to invest in a range of lines, enough reels and a decent collection of rods, from

Pirks of all sizes are vital in the sea angler's armouries.

133

something you might spin for mackerel with up to something on which you might use a pirk weighing 1lb for cod. I do think you need a bigger range of gear than is necessary for coarse fishing spinning. It's best to be prepared. Of course, if the objective is only bass or only mackerel, then it's easier. (The needs of the travelling sea angler I'll describe in the final chapter.)

Sea anglers have always had a huge range of lures available to them – all manner of spinners, 'flies', jigs, perks, sand eels, feathered hooks, and so on. In fact, when I first began sea fishing I found a bigger range of lures than was available specifically for pike anglers, so I used mackerel spinners for pike in shallow, weedy lakes, and rubber sand eels for pike all over the place. One of my first sea fish on lure was when I was out from the South Landing at Flamborough Head in a 12ft clinker-built dinghy. As well as bait on the bottom hook I had a mackerel spinner on a paternoster boom about 3ft above the lead. This is what the fish took and as I played it up from around 40ft down I thought it would weigh 10lb: it was a 1½lb codling. (On another occasion,

using the same method, I had a 1lb eel. That one didn't fight.)

The knots sea anglers use on their rigs are often a bit different to those used by the freshwater angler, but I always use half-blood knots and have never come to grief yet in terms of knots. However, I do feel you need better swivels than you'd use in freshwater: bigger, stronger, corrosion proof. They have to put up not only with twisting, powerful fish, but with sand, salt and seaweed. Get the best you can.

Take advice locally when it comes to leads. You may need lead to get the lure or perk down deep; or you may need lead to help when casting from the rocks or a beach. One thing I haven't seen sea anglers use much is the Dave Steuart salmon paternoster system (see Chapter 11), but it works well on any beach. I used it not long ago on a Spanish (Atlantic) beach after bass. I used a 3oz paternoster lead and short link, plus a floating plug. I set it so that the plug didn't come up to the surface, but watching it quite close in I could see it worked well so had no hesitation chucking it 60yd so or. Nor did it tangle up.

Australian cocky salmon, a pollack-like species, provides good eating as well as sport. This is one of a large bag taken on small wobbling spoons of concavo-convex profile.

A lot of bass anglers use Tobys or similar spoons in the surf, but on snag-free beaches such as those in Western Ireland, you can use heavier spoons and get real distance – it doesn't matter if the spoon 'puffs' the sand on the way in. In fact, it probably helps. In truth, though, I can't talk with authority on Irish bass because I've mostly caught pollack there. Pollack, and the similar coalfish, like me; bass don't. A lot of bass anglers use plugs off the rocks and in gullies and you can chase the wrasse in rocky gullies using jigs and spoons. In fact, in Tasmania, I did quite well with big wrasse using spinner-baits of ½–1oz. In other parts of Australia I've had a variety of species, including the pollack-like Australian or cocky salmon on spoons, plugs (that is, paternostered plugs) and small jigs. On one Australian sandy

Barrie fishing the surf.

beach, with scattered tabular rock, I took a 30lb common skate on a spinnerbait. It chased the lure in, clearly visible in the shallow, sandy water, and then pounced on it – but as it did so I think it saw me and turned rapidly away, but its wing caught the stinger treble of the spinnerbait. After not much of a battle, I beached it. For this kind of fishing a salmon or pike spinning rod will suffice, or a custom-built bass spinning rod, of course. Also, for this kind of lure fishing, I prefer a fixed spool reel. Many rate the multiplier more highly, but I can't really see why. But it's horses for courses; one of the pleasures of a multiplier is that the moment the lure hits the surface your left hand is on the reel and you are in full control, but with a fixed spool reel there is a split second of delay whilst you put the pick-up on. If you are in amongst rocks, you might think that immediate control was important.

As in all lure fishing, the choice of lure is important. It is true that when the mackerel are on the feed they'll take anything which looks like a fish. And I've had many large catches of small pollack off the rocks and piers in Western Ireland, when the fish seemed to hit anything. But big pollock and bass are a different matter altogether and whether its beach or boat it will be necessary to get the right lure. It follows that unless you have good local knowledge you need a range of lures in your bag. Take all the tried and trusted ones, for example rubber sand eels for bass and pollack off the boat, but also take others that you think might work if fished over a wreck. The fact that variety can work is proved by the changing fashions that sea anglers go through. I remember one fad for perks for Yorkshire cod fishing – everybody used them, swore by them, but I caught more on jigged rubber worms. Today, I'd make sure I dipped those rubber worms in a juicy mix of something before lowering them over the side. Sea anglers in the UK don't seem to add taste to their lures,

Pollack country.

or additives such as a ragworm or lugworm, but they do elsewhere in the world. The exception is the baited spoon for flounder fishing where a hook or two (singles as a rule), trailing behind the egg-shaped spoon blade, will have a worm attachment. I once found that white plastic spoons seemed to work better than silver-coloured metal spoons, but you needed enough lead to hold it down on the sand.

In summary, the coarse or game fisherman should try mentally to move himself away from freshwater thinking, especially in terms of rods. The work is sometimes – often – heavier on the tackle so you need to upgrade accordingly. It is better if one buys specialist corrosion-proof sea reels: freshwater reels work well but need serious washing and re-oiling after every trip. With proper sea reels you can give them, and the line, a quick rinse. Rods need wiping down after a session with a wet cloth and then dried off. Salt is a menace on anything, and salt out of sight can destroy mechanisms and glues. Get a big range of lure types, everything from feathered hooks to big perks, and remember, too, that these will also need a good rinse in freshwater after use.

Wrasse country. This is a little foolhardy. The gear is inadequate. Good boots, a lifejacket and a big rod would help!

136

16 Flies and Lures

This is not to be a chapter wholly about fly-casting lures for predatory fish, though there is no reason why a suitable fly rod cannot be used for chucking many lures, both small and quite large (*see* picture of pike 'flies'). It's more to make the point, one of the threads running through this book, that lures grade one into another. Earlier, I discussed how some of Waltham's sea trout 'flies' were really small plugs disguised with feathers and hair. There's nothing at all wrong with this, of course. It's almost only a matter of terminology; although if one calls it a fly, rather than a spinner or a plug, I guess it's easier to get permission to put it on the water. That is a philosophical problem very well dealt with by Fred J. Taylor in Chapter 12. Like Fred, I'm more

concerned with the practical fishing side of these hybrid lures (even that word is ambiguous isn't it?) rather than morals or sportsmanship, both of which reside in the angler, not the rule book.

I suppose pike fishing is the other area where fly fishing has caught on (*see* 'Useful Addresses' for details of the Pike Fly-Fishing Association). It went through teething problems but a kind of consensus now operates. A few serious anglers, such as Des Taylor, don't like the idea of *summer* fly fishing for pike (or, indeed, summer lure fishing for pike), but I must say that if the gear is right and the angler's attitude is right it cannot really do much harm, if any. That has been my own experience with both forms of summer fishing, even though,

Billed as pike flies, these also catch many predators.

137

nowadays, most of my fly fishing for pike is in winter, on the Fenland drains, where I do not suffer from backcast problems or distance-casting problems.

The truth is that for pike fly fishing the rod should be powerful, say 10–12 weight (mine are 12 weight). The lines should be appropriate to that and the monofil leader, of 4–6ft only, needs to be of around 18lb bs. With gear like that you can bully pike to the bank in summer just as quickly as you can with pike spinning gear (or, indeed, pike deadbait gear). The important word is 'bully'. I see too many anglers barely leaning into their fish at all, even on 3lb tc rods, unnecessarily prolonging the fight. To put a semicircle in a 3lb tc rod needs a pull of only 3lb or a little more, so how on earth can a line of 18lb bs be at risk? The truth is it cannot. So give the fish some welly. If you do that it will be on the bank quickly and you can return it quickly.

You need a wire trace. The best ones are about 9in long, of piano wire or equivalent. They should be stiff and as long as you can cast; 6in is a little too short sometimes. The kinds of wires used for deadbaiting are not really suitable because they twist and kink too easily. Some of those you can tie knots in might be okay, but I haven't yet used them so cannot comment. The famous Dutch pike fly angler Ad Swier came up with the right answer, as he does so often, namely a wire trace with a spiral coil at the business end which obviates the need for a link swivel. (Link swivels are fine in principle, but they add a lot of weight to the lure.) The number of coils in Ad's traces is enough to ensure that fish twisting as they fight do not unlock the trace. I've used exactly this tackle on big Nile perch, which also spiral and twist during the fight, and even there the flies/lures did not come adrift. And that is a big test of a trace.

Now we come to the lures. Disparaging remarks have often been made about pike flies/lures, including the comment that casting some of them is like chucking a drowned parrot. This is not far from the truth either. Some of these lures, when wet, act like a dishcloth in the air, falling on the water for all the world like a dead parrot. The initial answer, again pioneered by Ad Swier, was to use materials in the tying of the lures that was extremely light and/or water repelling: I have put some of these in the

A full fly box. Note the Ad Swier wire trace with its spiral connector instead of a link swivel.

Barrie fly fishing a bug in one of Tasmania's Great Lakes, where he had some nice browns in inches of water.

A big pike on fly from the Old Bedford River.

illustration opposite. But in the first decade of this millennium it became clearer that big so-called flies were not all that necessary for pike and even big pike will take smaller lures. Nowadays, pike fly anglers often use flies – and we can almost call them that – of 1–4in in length, often quite sparsely furnished.

If these flies have diving vanes or spinning blades one can really only call them plugs and spinners and any angler keen on this kind of fishing might move from one to the other during the day (as might a sea trout angler (*see* Chapter 13). Furthermore, these smaller lures can be cast with a spinning rod just as well as with a powerful fly rod. So, full circle … and as the lures themselves get smaller and smaller, go back to Chapter 8. Everything in lure fishing grades into everything else. None is more or less sporting than any other, though on the day one method may be more successful than the others. Or, and this is important too, a

particular method may give more pleasure to the angler than other methods and he'll take the reduction in efficiency on board as part of the price of his pleasure.

I should mention another way of fishing these large flies-cum-lures than with a fly rod, and that is by fishing them beneath a former – a dark, heavy float-like tapered cylinder which you can use either as a floater or as a sinker. If you sink it to the bottom and the lure is buoyant, just imagine how you can work it down in the depths. I have used this technique for many years and it really does work.

Let me tell you of two preferred circumstances. Imagine a large, still water, that is shallow and with heavy weed growth reaching up to about 3ft below the surface – in other words, an early season scenario on many of our waters. If you use the former (a floater) at 2ft 6in above the lure, then the lure can never sink into the thick weed and you can work it sink and draw over huge areas. It's a killing method and I have taken many pike, perch and trout like this. The downside is that the fish sometimes maul the former instead of the lure. (I have a former with a wire trace through it and hooks on it.)

The lure itself for this fishing need not be one of these pike fly/lures but can be a smaller, true fly, or a spinner, spoon or plug – or one of these adorned with a fly. They all work. The fish, naturally, are sitting in the thick weed cover, looking upwards for food, and pike especially come up like Polaris missiles. Other fish, too, fall to this method, such as rudd and roach and sometimes bream (and *see* Chapter 8).

The second circumstance where the method is good is when you cannot *cast* downstream to where you want to the lure to be. Therefore you *float* it down, using a floating former. You can send it a hundred yards if you like and the lure can be anything you fancy. You are constrained only by the depth at which you have to set the lure to avoid snags, weeds, shallows or whatever. I have found this quite a good way of poaching someone else's water – at least a hundred yards of it. Obviously it works well on rivers and can be excellent at dealing with a difficult bend or overgrown banks. If you use drifter float you can even use the technique on lakes (the former itself doesn't blow too well because of the drag of the lure hanging below it). One advantage of this method over using a fly rod or spin casting is that a 'dead parrot' can be chucked more easily.

This concept of lures and techniques that are transitional between one tradition or style can be considered further. For example,

what is a spinnerbait? The name itself gives you a clue: we don't know. It does not really fit into the traditional categories of spinner, spoon, plug or fly. The blade is spoon-like, true, but it flutters. And, more importantly, prey such as a pike, when it strikes, does not target the spoon blade, but the skirt. I have observed this many times with small pike, zander and trout; they go for the skirt. Of course, when a big fish takes you cannot tell which bit of the lure it is after, because the whole lure may be in the fish's mouth, but if it is the skirt which is primarily being targeted, are we fly fishing? Incidentally, whenever I have lost the spoon blade from a spinnerbait I have continued to catch on the skirt alone, but I suspect at a reduced rate.

We don't need to get too hung up on all this, though, do we? That said, it is important to realize that the addition or subtraction of something from a lure can markedly affect results. So we shouldn't hesitate to try a bit of fly-tying material on spinners (as in the old-fashioned fly spoons), on plugs or on spoons. On the last of these the material needs to be added very carefully to avoid detracting from the action of the spoon. I usually dress such additions on a trailing or stinger treble.

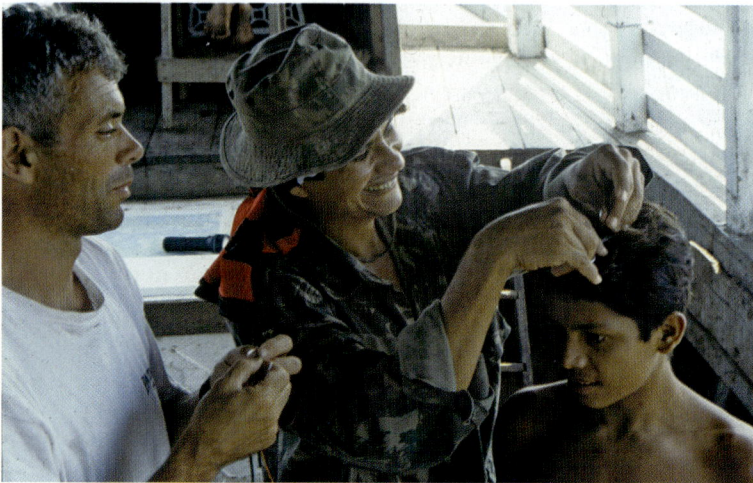

Josimar, watched by Jeremy Wade, removes some of Espanch's hair to make a fly for Arawana. It produced an 8lb fish!

17 The Travelling Lure Angler

One of the greatest pleasures awaiting the new lure fisherman – and many old hands too perhaps – is that of fishing around the world in a huge variety of circumstances. You don't have to be travelling with fishing in mind; it may be a work trip, a conference or a family holiday, but go prepared and you can have some splendid fishing which often gives a welcome break from what you were supposed to be doing. I have taken my travelling spinning kit and fished in many places: Siberia for Arctic char and grayling; St Petersburg for ruff; Argentina (the Andes) for brown trout; the Amazon for peacock bass, piranha and other fish; Canada for anything; Norway and Sweden for trout, perch and pike; France for trout; Spain for bass; many parts of Australia for both sea and freshwater fish including wild rainbows, and the Great Barrier Reef for trevally and other species.

I usually carry a couple of telescopics. One will be fairly powerful, maybe with a 3lb test curve, but short; the other will be a 6–8ft wand that one would normally think of using for trout spinning or small pike. Normally I carry one good fixed spool reel with two or three spools. The spools will carry a light line, say 6–8lb bs monofil (or a heavier braid) and the others heavier bs in braids. That's about all you need. You can buy leads, hooks and lures – especially lures – in most places in the world, but you cannot always get hold of a decent rod and reel. Local lures can be quite different to those you are used to. For example,

in Australia the Tasmanian Devil was a favourite lure which casts well. It has an erratic, darting retrieve, like a high-speed jerkbait. You can now get them in the UK under various names, but until I brought a batch back with me nobody had seen them here. I caught a lot of different freshwater and marine species on them, but do not think they are particularly better than many other lures.

However, I have to say that I do take a few favourite lures with me, including distance-casting spoons, though not necessarily large ones. I always carry a couple

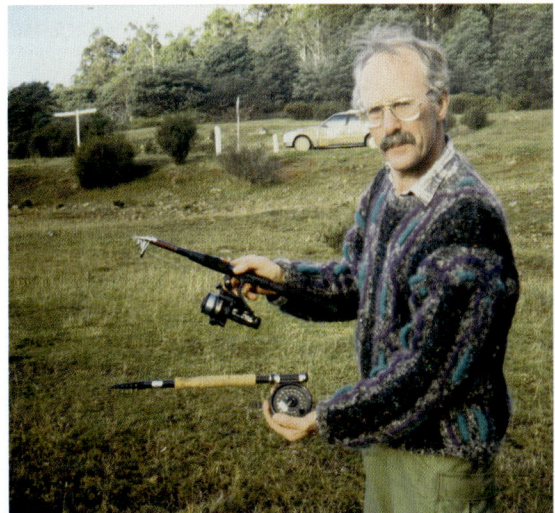

Barrie's travelling kit, which goes all the world over. A telescopic spinning rod and a 9-weight fly rod.

141

Big black piranha. Both fish and angler have their teeth hidden on this shot.

of Barrie's Buzzer spinnerbaits because of their versatility in so many situations. I mentioned in Chapter 15 getting some big Australian wrasse on them. This was classic South West England wrasse country: deep, seaweed-fringed gullies in surf-battered rocky points. I used the spinnerbait with a single hook only, chucked it into the gullies and let it sink to the bottom – then retrieved either by jigging or sink and draw. Wrasse fight well and it was hectic sport at times. I had one wrasse species up to 3½lb which wasn't that far short of the Australian record at the time for that species.

Another lure I always carry is something like a Toby, because they cast like bullets and yet can be fished shallow or deep. Sometimes I take a hammer to them and beat them so that they have more of

Good peacock bass from the Brazilian Amazon.

Peacock bass in all its glory.

142

an undulating, concavo-convex shape, which gives them a better wobble on the retrieve. I remember one day on Wineglass Bay in Tasmania – it's a surf beach with a steep slope into deep water – I was using the light telescopic, 6lb bs monofil and a 4in, heavy, wobbling Toby. Because the bottom sloped steeply down to 30ft or so, the undertow going out to sea was tremendous. If you retrieved immediately the lure hit the surface of the sea – always worth a try – then the lure came back fast and shallow. To fish deeper it was necessary to let out a lot of loose line quickly as the lure hit the sea, and this you can do easily by raising the rod to the vertical, with the pick up open, then lowering the rod quickly. This allows the lure to sink very quickly through the surface layers of water, which are being driven towards the beach, and

A good Tigerfish from Lake Nasser in Egypt.

into the deeper water which is flowing away from the beach. Once you have tightened up the line you then find you are retrieving, slowly, against the current. It proved deadly and produced for me my biggest Australian salmon of 6lb and that on a line of 6lb bs. The fish gave a tremendous battle, repeatedly taking out line at depth, until I finally got it nearer the surface. It wasn't finished: I watched it swimming at high speed just under the very crest of the wave, before the wave broke. Eventually it lost the battle as a particularly large breaker dumped the fish on the beach and it lay stranded as the water raced away from it. And all that because, whilst travelling and working, I had with me the kind of lightweight tackle kit described at the beginning of the chapter.

When you are packing tackle in this way, perhaps into the family suitcase, it adds little to the weight or bulk and you are tempted to add other items. Don't. The crucial things in lure fishing are rod, reel and line. The rest can be obtained almost anywhere you go. I do wrap up both reel and travelling rods in a bit of bubble plastic because you don't want them damaged in transit. I used to carry reels in my hand baggage on flights, but in these security-conscious times this is not so easy.

Perhaps the only item of tackle I have occasionally needed, and regretted not taking, is split shot. Large shot enables you to fish light/small lures and get a decent cast out of them. For example, whilst working on the rocks of New South Wales, Australia (near the town of Orange), I got into a bit of wild rainbow trout fishing, made available by a friendly farmer. The most successful lures were tiny bar spoons, the smallest ones made by Mepps and Shakespeare (both purchased at a tackle shop in Sydney). As it happened, I'd taken out about a dozen swan shots of the non-toxic variety and these were fixed to the

Barrie stalking peacock bass on a backwater of the Amazon.

very swivel of the lure, not only giving distance but helping to prevent line twists. The trout stream had small, deep pools, up to 6ft deep, separated by long, shallow riffles. When I was there the trout were deep in the pools, beneath gum tree roots, so the lure had to go down quickly or else work in from the tail of the pool, diving as it went. Effective retrieve distance was possibly three to four yards – and it worked well, with quite a few nice, pan-sized rainbows. Of course, in Europe you don't have

to worry about substitute lead because fishing leads are not banned as in the UK. And you could always make a small lead weight out of sheet lead if necessary.

Another typical experience occurred in the Andes Mountains of San Juan Province in Argentina. We were on an international geological field trip and travelling by coach alongside the San Juan River, through its gorges. At intervals we stopped to tap rocks. At lunchtime we stopped high above the river, but beneath towering and

In the Russian Arctic, chasing char and grayling.

Adventurers in lure fishing on the Amazon.

majestic mountains. I decided to eat my packed lunch on the move somewhere, but to use the lunch hour – just an hour, no more – to cast a line in the gorge below. I just happened to have, in my backpack, a telescopic fly rod and a tiny telescopic spinning rod of 7ft. Lures were either flies or small spoons. I decided to hedge my bets, chose the spinning rod, but picked a spinner with a tail fly attached. I'd heard it was a trout river.

At that point the San Juan River is a mighty river, at 9,000ft above sea level, all fast water, with eddies and bare rocks, sand bars and gravel spits. Casting was tricky because the lure was swept at high speed whatever one seemed to do. After several retrieves which were, in effect, very shallow, I came up with a cunning plan. I added a little lead in the form of two swan shots to the very eye region of the lure, chucked it upstream and across as far as I could, and then left it on a loose line to sink. When I began the retrieve there was a huge downsteam bow in the line. The lure came in deeper, banged on a rock and then reached the bank. I was puzzled about the rock because the lure was nowhere near the bottom.

So I chucked it out again. This time, in exactly the same place, the rock transformed itself into a fish and I had a fight on my hands with 6lb bs line in a powerful current. But I beached the fish eventually by allowing it to drift backwards, downsteam of me – then ran and grabbed it. It was a lovely brownie of around 3lb weight, but very short, fat and as deep as a bream. In the meantime the boss had seen

Two youngsters, one a piranha.

145

Barrie spinning on the San Juan River in the Argentine Andes.

A nice brownie on fly/spoon at 9,000ft in the Argentine Andes. (Photograph courtesy of Mandy Lyne)

what was happening, so she ran down the slope of the hill, fitting a telephoto lens as she ran, and managed to get a picture of me with the fish just before I slid it back. She had already taken one of me fishing, a mere pin prick of a human in an awe-inspiring setting.

On the other side of the globe I had some interesting experiences in the (old) Soviet Arctic, in the Kolyma Peninsula. My journey there had had its problems, not least being getting visas from one town to the next. Finally, I got a lift on a Soviet Army helicopter from Magadan to the field camp on the Kolyma. I think the local geologists were somewhat surprised when the army helicopter landed at their camp and divested, not soldiers, but a geologist. Each day we rock-tapped in the tundra, which involved long walks along glacial streams, and each day I carried in my backpack a telescopic spinning rod. But there wasn't the opportunity or time for a cast and so finally I left the tackle at the camp. Of course, that was the day when the opportunity arose …

In the nick of time. The biter almost bit.

We were sitting at lunch, some distance from any rivers, when another army helicopter hove into view, clearly looking for us. On landing, they demanded my presence. Naturally both I and the rest of the party thought I was being arrested for something. Not a bit of it: it turned out that the first helicopter pilot, learning I was an angler, had arranged to fly me to a fisherman's camp about 100km into the tundra. So off I went (wondering whether I'd ever see civilization again). The camp had temporary tents – yurt-like constructions – and three or four Russian enthusiasts. Their method was to dry the catch, salt it and bag it, then take it home and both use it for food and sell it on. How I wish I'd had my telescopic and fixed spool reel. As it was, I had to spin with a tin (possibly aluminium) centre pin which took a while to get used to. But we caught Arctic char and grayling averaging 1–2½lb and when the Russians finally flew me back to our camp they donated a whole sackful of salted char and grayling for our camp chef. I'd love to return there some day because the scenery is as spectacular as the fishing. There's not a vestige of weed, not a scrap of cover, only glacially polished and washed blue boulders, sand bars and gravel – and swims full of Arctic char and grayling.

Trolling on ... Barrie, Geoff Neville and Russell Manning, watched by Tim Baily, troll into the dark.

Bibliography

Bailey, J., *In Wild Waters* (The Crowood Press, 1989)

Barder, R.C.R., *Spinning for Pike* (David & Charles, 1970)

Batten, D., *An Introduction to Pike Fishing* (The Crowood Press, 1989)

Bettell, C., *The Art of Lure Fishing* (The Crowood Press, 1994)

Bickerdyke, J., *Angling for Pike* (Upcott Gill, 1888)

Buller, F., *Pike* (MacDonald & Co., 1971)

Carter Platts, W., *Modern Trout Fishing* (Adam & Charles Black, 1938)

Cooper, A.E. (ed.), *Sea Fishing: The Lonsdale Library Volume 17* (Seeley Service & Co. Ltd, 1935)

Darling, J., *Bass Fishing on Shore and Sea* (The Crowood Press, 1996)

Fox, C.K., *The Book of Lures* (Fresnet Press, 1975)

Gammon, C., *Hook, Line and Spinner* (William Heinemann, 1959)

Greer, R., *Ferox Trout and Arctic Charr* (Swan Hill Press, 1995)

Hanna, A., *Fly Fishing for Big Pike* (Coch-y-Bonddu Books, 1998)

Hansen, J.P. & Cederberg, G., *Spinning and Baitcasting* (Swann Hill Press, 1994)

Harris, S. & C., *Encyclopaedia of Lures* (The Crowood Press, 1993)

Holgate, J., *Big Water Pike Fishing Book 1* (Cast Publications, 1989)

Holgate, J., *Big Water Pike Fishing Book 2* (Cast Publications, 1990)

Holgate, J., *Catching Pike on Lures* (Cast Publications, 1991)

Holgate, J., (ed.), *Lure Fishing for Pike: Vol. 1* (Cast Publications, 1987)

Holgate, J., (ed.), *Lure Fishing for Pike: Vol. 2* (Cast Publications, 1988)

Holgate, J. et al., *Catch Pike with Lures* (Predator Publications Ltd, 2007)

Holiday, F.W., *River Fishing for Sea Trout* (Herbert Jenkins, 1960)

Housby, T., *Sea Fishing* (The Crowood Press, 1991)

Housby, T., *An Introduction to Sea Fishing* (The Crowood Press, 1992)

Housby, T., *The Art of Sea Angling* (Evans Brothers Ltd, 1996)

Howes, W.J., *Spinning for Coarse, Sea and Game Fish* (W. Foulsham, 1962)

Ladle, M. & Casey, H., *A New Approach to Lure Fishing* (A. & C. Black, 1988)

Luckey, C.F., *Old Fishing Lures and Tackle* (Books Americana, 1980)

McEwan, W., *Angling on Lomond* (Albyn Press Ltd, 1980)

Oglesby, A., *Salmon* (Macdonald & Co. Ltd, 1971)

Pritchard, M., *Pocket Guide to Spinning in Fresh and Saltwater* (Collins, 1984)

Rickards, B., *Pike Fishing Step by Step* (Cassell, 1976)

Rickards, B., *Freshwater Fishing* (Transeditons Ltd, 1991) [translation and new edition of *La Pêche et ses Techniques* (France Loisirs)]

Rickards, B., *Success with the Lure* (Video Active, 1991), DVD and Video

Rickards, B., *In Search of Nile Perch* (Video Active, 2001), DVD and Video

Rickards, B. & Whitehead, K., *Plugs and Plug Fishing* (A. & C. Black, 1976)

Rickards, B. & Whitehead, K., *Spinners, Spoons and Wobbled Baits* (A. & C. Black, 1977)

Rickards, B. & Whitehead, K., *Spinning and Plug Fishing* (A. & C. Black, 1987)

Rickards, B. & Bannister, M., *The Great Modern Pike Anglers* (The Crowood Press, 2007)

Scott, J., *Sea Trout Fishing: The Lonsdale Library Volume 35* (Seeley, Service & Co. Ltd, 1969)

Scott, J., *Spinning Up to Date* (Seeley, Service & Co. Ltd, 1937)

Spence, E., *The Pike Fisher* (A. & C. Black, 1928)

Spencer, S., *Pike on the Plug* (Witherby, 1936)

Stoker, H. (ed.), *Sea Angling with the Specimen Hunters* (Ernest Benn Ltd, 1977)

Swier, A., *Passion for Pike* (Drukkerij Westerlaan, Lichtenvoorde with Coch-y-Bonddu Books, 2006)

Thurlow-Craig, C., *Spinner's Delight.* (Hutchinson Library, 1951)

Thurlow-Craig, C., *Baitmaker's Delight.* (Hutchinson Library, 1953)

Veale, S., *Fishing Lures: A Practical Guide* (Sportsman Press, 1992)

Waddington, R., *On Salmon Fishing.* (The Crowood Press, 1991)

Waltham, J., *The Sea Trout and the Fly* (The Crowood Press, 2006)

Webb, R. & Rickards, B., *Fishing for Big Pike* (A. & C. Black, 1971)

Useful Addresses

The Lure Anglers' Society
By Eric Weight

The first and perhaps most obvious thing to say about the Lure Anglers' Society (LAS) is that it is not a species-orientated society. Our members fish for anything and everything from asp to zander, just so long as it can be fooled into taking an artificial lure.

Our full-colour quarterly magazine carries articles on coarse, sea and game fishing, in both this country and abroad. We send magazines to subscribers in Canada, the USA, Japan, Singapore, Spain and Sweden. Many members are as interested in making and modifying lures as they are in using them and the magazine is a great source of inspiration for those interested in pushing the boundaries of their lure fishing beyond what can be bought over the counter.

We have regular fish-ins and competitions throughout the year which give members the chance to meet and fish with other lure anglers and compare tackle and tactics. These are held at venues as diverse as gravel pits, major rivers, canals, drains and reservoirs. They are great opportunities to try different styles of lure fishing and to see how others approach these waters.

The LAS has a very strong social side, driven in part by the fish-ins and in recent times by its active Internet forum. Numerous small fish-ins take place during the season. They are organized by the members themselves via the Internet and these are great ways to meet fellow lure anglers and to share knowledge. Many strong friendships have developed from these events and a lot more fish have been caught using new techniques and lures discovered on these days.

Above all, the LAS aims to restore something that has been gradually disappearing from the modern angling scene – fun. Big fish/small fish, it doesn't matter to our members just so long as they are enjoying their fishing.

Why not come and join in? Visit our website at: www.lureanglers.co.uk for more information.

At the time of writing (2008) membership is £17 per annum with concessions for families, juniors, the unemployed and senior citizens. Contact the LAS at either of the following addresses:

Bob Tweedle
15 Crane Ley Road
Groby
Leicestershire

LE6 0FD
Tel: 0116 291 4776
e-mail: membership@lureanglers.co.uk

Eric Weight
43 Station Road
Higham on the Hill
Nr Nuneaton
Warwickshire
CV13 6AG
Tel: 01455 212679
e-mail: editor@lureanglers.co.uk

Other Useful Addresses

The Bass Anglers' Sportfishing Society
Secretary
Frank Whittingham
Shawe Cottage
Shawe
Kingsley Holt
Cheadle
ST10 2DL

The National Mullet Club
Ben Mullins
Flat 1
38 Sackville Road
Hove
BN3 3FB
Tel: 01273 728410

The Pike Anglers' Club (PAC), founded in 1977, is another active body with many lure anglers as members and with numerous activities and a very successful quarterly magazine called *Pikelines*.
Membership Secretary
John Cahill
312 Hobs Moat Road
Solihull
B92 8JX
Tel. 05601 313753 (7–9pm)
e-mail: memberships@pacgb.co.uk

The PAC forum is pacgb.co.uk/message-board.htm

The Perchfishers is another active club which will welcome perch lure enthusiasts.
The contact is Steve Richards on 01462 480353.

The International Game Fishing Association (IGFA) can be contacted via David Bird (*see* Chapter 14) at:
33 Manor Road South
Hinchley Wood
Surrey
KT10 OQ4
Fax: 0181 398 9267

Pike and Predators is a monthly magazine that lure anglers should not miss. Many of the new techniques and discoveries appear here first. You can send your name, address and relevant details to: Predator Publications (Subscriptions), Newport, East Yorkshire, HU15 2QG or telephone same to 01430 440624 (Fax 01430 441319). If in difficulty e-mail: pikeandpredators@btopenworld.com

Useful Addresses for Fishing Holidays Abroad (*see* Chapter 14)

Tailor Made Holidays – www.tailormade-holidays.co.uk – Tel: 020 8398 7424

Worldwide Fishing Safaris – www.world-widefishingsafaris.co.uk – Tel: 01733 271123

World Sport Fishing – www.worldsport-fishing.com – Tel: 01480 403293

Dial-A-Flight – www.dialaflight.com – Tel: 0870 333 4488. This company will also arrange hotel accommodation, car hire, and so on. They are not fishing specialists.

Jerkbait Rods

Because these are rather specialized rods I suggest you could make a good start by looking at Dave Lumb's stable on www.dlst.co.uk, where he also has many items of tackle suitable for the lure angler.

There remain two very useful organizations to mention; both are useful for the lure angler. One is the Pike Fly Fishing Association (*see* Chapter 16), established primarily to cater for anglers wishing to use fly fishing techniques for pike. However, many of its members use the techniques to fish for other predatory species too. Points of contact are: pffachairman@btinternet.co.uk, or PFFA, 28 Crown Avenue, Holbeach St Marks, Spalding, Lincs PE12 8FU. The website is: www.pffa.co.uk. The organization runs various events during the year, has a newsletter and merchandise, and so on.

The second organization, and one supported by most of the above bodies, is the Specialist Anglers' Alliance (SAA). As its name implies, it represents, at all levels, the interests of specialist groups, including all lure fishers. The best point of contact is the Secretary, Mike Heylin, at mike@heylin.com. The SAA has a long evolutionary history. In the 1960s the specialist angling groups combined into a National Association of Specimen Groups (NASG). This later divided into angling and political wings (NASG and SACG or Specialist Angling Conservation Group). Later still they recombined to form the SAA, the vibrant and active body we have today. Lure anglers do run into problems now and then – of access, of allowable techniques, for example – and the SAA is probably their first port of call.

An envelope sent to the author by a lure fishing enthusiast!

Index

Abbey Mill Fishery   93, 116
ABU 5000/6000   72
Africa, East   126, 127
Amazon, River   87, 145
amberjack   122, 126, 129
Andes Mountains, Argentina   144, 146
anti-kink vanes and leads   23, 25, 35, 85
Arawana   87, 140
Ardingly Reservoir   105
Argentina   141
Arkaig, Loch   77
Atlantic spoon   76
Awe, Loch   72, 107

babydolls   16
Baily, Tim   147
ball-bearing swivels   41, 62
Ballyquirke, Loch   72
banana lure or wobbler   16, 24
Bannister, Malcolm   20, 42, 61
Barrie's Buzzer   25, 28, 142
barspoons   18, 19, 23, 24, 25, 87, 89, 112, 117
bass   34, 132, 133, 134, 135
Bass Anglers' Sportfishing Society   151
Bassenthwaite Lake   72
Baxter, Jim   88
Believer lure   39, 76
bug lures   49
Big N   76
Big S   18, 29, 45
Bionic Buctail lure   76
Bird, Maggi   120
Black Magdawg lure   71
boats   48, 49
Bomber LA   76

bottom lumping retrieve   78
braid   33, 36, 61, 63, 69, 72
bream (bronze)   83, 85, 86
Bridlington   132
Brown, Mick   21
Brute lure   76
Bulldawg-style   18, 21, 47, 67, 90
Buller, Fred   110
Burmek lure   63
buzzers   18, 19, 25, 26, 27

Cabelas, Nebraska, USA   42
camo clothing   37
Cannon down-rigger   71
carp   88
celluloid-vaned flight   96
centre pin reels   103
char   110, 141, 144, 147
chub   63, 81, 83, 84, 86, 87
Cisco Kid lure   71, 75
coalfish   135
cod   125, 132, 133
Cole, Tim   29
Colorado spoon   13, 22, 84
concavo-convex lure/spoon   143
Coniston Water   72
Conn, Lough   68
Corrib, Lough   68, 105
Cortland   72
countdowns   16, 20, 78
crankbaits   14, 16, 18, 24, 30, 44, 88, 108
crayfish (lures)   84, 87
Crazy Crawler   17, 18
Creek Chub Pike lure   43, 72, 76, 89
Crowther, Peter   81

Delph river   90, 118
Depth charts   78
Depth Raider lures   41, 68, 71, 72, 76, 77, 78
Dail-a-Flight   152
diving vane   119
downrigger   71, 75
drag/clutch   79
drift fishing with lures   58
drop-offs   59

East Africa   120
echo sounders   49, 74
eels   88
eels, rubber   21
Egypt   37, 38, 66
electric lures   31
electric motors   59
engines   52, 53
Ennel, Lough   68
Ernie   17, 75, 77
Ernie lure, Big   74
Espanch   140
experimental lures   30

Fenland   40, 62, 118, 138
ferox trout   68, 69, 77
Fireline   72
fish finders   55, 56
Fitzgibbon, Stuart   130
fixed cabin boat   52
fixed spool reels   36, 103, 133, 135
Flasher lure   76
floating diving plugs   16
floating plugs   17, 20
flounder   136
Flying Condom   29
fly spoons   23, 24
forceps   33, 41
formers   46, 139
Fox   42, 63
freeboard   50
frog lures   40

gaffs   42
Garnafailagh, Lough, Ireland   85

Gator-Back lure   76
Gloveri, Peter   127
Gould, Steve   14
GPS   56
Grandma lure   71, 72, 76
grasshopper, plastic   24
grayling   147
Great Barrier Reef, Australia   17, 141
Great Lakes, Tasmania   139
Great Ouse, River   87, 90, 118
Grinder lure   76
groynes   93
Gudebrod Sniper lure   105

Hall, Colin   90
Hampshire Avon, River   94, 97, 104
Heath, Linda   130
Hedgehog   18, 19, 61
Hellcats Magnum lure   72
Hellier, Robbie   126, 129
Hemingways Resort, Kenya   126, 127, 129
Henry's Lake, Idaho, USA   109
Honda   53
Hooker lure   74, 76
hook-out   41
hull, Cathedral   51
hull, displacement   51
hull, planing   51

internal layout (boats)   54
International Game Fishing Association
    (IGFA)   128, 151
Itchen, River   91

Jardine leads   79, 97
jerkbaits   16, 18, 20, 62, 63, 107, 151
jerkbaits, mini   20
jigs   18, 19, 20, 21, 24, 66, 89, 90
Jimbo lure   117

Kelbrick, Dave   61
Ken, Loch   68, 72, 74, 79
Kennet, River   115
Kenya   125, 128
kidney spoon   13, 23

Kilty Lures   29
Kite, Oliver   106
K12 Kwikfish   28
kiting (salmon fishing)   98
Kolyma Peninsula, Russia   146
Kunsamo Professor   76

Lake District   77, 106
Lake of the Woods, Canada   78
landing nets   33, 34, 42
Lark, River   118
lead-cored line   71, 74
leads, in-line   71, 76
leads, snap-on   71, 76
leads, up-trace   112
leister   107
line indicators   83
Lomond, Loch   72, 105
Loz Harrop's Darter lure   77
Lucky Strike Lizard   23
Lumb, Dave   8, 61, 151
Lune, River   116
Lure Anglers' Society (LAS)   10, 50
lure boxes   44
lure colours   77
lure retrieval system   73
lure size   76
Lyne, Mandy   146

mackerel   119, 125, 134, 135
mackerel, frigate, "friggies"   130
mackerel spinners   22, 23, 25, 46, 132, 133
Magadan, Russia   146
Manning, Russel   147
Mann's Stretch   25, 72
Marlin   36, 131
Mask, Lough   68, 73, 80, 110
Mepps, Europe   44
Mepps lures   15, 24, 82, 88, 94, 98, 99, 143
microbarbs   43
micromesh nets   42, 43
Middy S   45, 89
Milford, John   8
minnows   23, 25, 95, 96, 97, 99, 100, 101,
    112

Mitchell reels   103
Mono (monofil)   69
Monster Shad lure   77
'Mountains, The', Kenya   130
Muchno, Loch   72, 76
Mullet Club, The National   151
multipliers   33, 36, 61, 62, 64, 72, 103, 133, 135
multirod use   74
muskies (muskelunge)   69

Nasser, Lake   66, 143
Neville, Geoff   147
New South Wales, Australia   82, 143
night spinning   89
Nile perch   20, 36, 37, 61, 66, 125, 138
Nilsmaster Invincible   17, 76
Norfolk Broads   28
Norwich spoon   13, 22, 23, 28, 86, 89, 105

Oich Loch   72
Old Bedford River   90, 139
Olivetti weights   83
Ondex lures   24
outrigger rod rest   72, 85

paternostering   45, 91, 93, 94, 97, 135
peacock bass   86, 141, 142
perch   63, 66, 67, 68, 77, 81, 83, 84, 85
Pike and Predators   10, 48, 151
Pike Anglers' Club (PAC)   10, 151
Piker spoon   28, 79
Pike Fly Fishing Association   152
Pikko lures   27
piranhas, red-bellied   86, 141, 142, 145
pirks   21, 24, 127, 128, 130, 132, 133, 134
planers (*see* side planers)
playing salmon   102
pliers   33, 41
Plough lure   76
Plucky Bait lure   84
plugs   22, 44
pollack   34, 125, 132, 133, 135, 136
polystickles   16
poppers   14, 18, 44, 119
puffer fish   66

quill minnow   13

Rapala Magnum lure   70, 75
Rapal Magnum countdown lure   71
Rapala Super Shad Rap   15, 77
Red Eye Wriggler lure   76
Ree, Lough   68
Relief Channel, cut-off, Great Ouse   90
Relief Channel, Great Ouse   90
Renosty lures   27, 89
Revett, Phil   129, 130
Robbins, Leslie   77, 106
rod holders   51, 57, 58
rubber lures   20, 21
rudd   83
Russelure   16
Russian Arctic   144, 146
Ryobi   26, 34

sailfish   127, 130, 131
Salmo lures   16, 20, 62
Salmo trutta   116
salmon   69, 92, 135, 136
salmon 'lies'   92
sandeel   133
St Petersburg, Russia   141
San Juan River, Argentina   144, 146
Scarborough   132
Sea Hog (boats)   52
sea trout   69
Shakespeare Co (UK) Ltd   15, 63, 143
Sheffield Angling Telegraph   88
Shimano Moocher Plus 4000GT   72, 73
shrimp, plastic   125
Siberia   141
Sibley, Alan   130
side planers   69, 70, 72
sink and draw   142
sinking plugs   16, 20
skate, common   135
Skee, Loch   72
small rivers, salmon   99
snake fly   117
snap-on leads   35
snapper   130

sonic rooster tail spinner   28
Specialist Anglers' Alliance (SAA)   152
spinnerbaits   18, 19, 25, 26, 27, 29, 76, 90,
   135, 140
spinners   21, 23
spinning, orthodox   96
spinning upstream   98
spoons   14, 28, 76, 85, 89, 136
sprats   95
squid, bulb   125
static lure fishing   59
stinger trebles   26, 140
storage of lures   31
Stor-Treen, Lake   71
Stour, River   94, 97, 104
streamer fly   115
striking   79, 100
Sturt, Ben   127
summer lure fishing   46
surface lures   18, 19, 89, 199
Swier, Ad   62, 138
Swift, Deryck (*see* Whitehead, Ken)   23
swivels   41, 43, 62, 63, 76, 93, 134

tandem lures   27
Tailor Made Holidays   152
Tasmanian Devil lure   141
Taylor, Des   137
Taylor, Fred J.   26, 38, 106, 137
techniques   36
temperatures, water   91
tench   83, 88
Ten Mile Bank, River, Great Ouse   87
test curve (tc)   32
Test, River   94, 97, 104
T. G. Lure Company   10, 14
Thames Water (Authority)   109
Thomas, Ben   130
tigerfish   20, 36, 61, 143
tiller   52
Toby spoons   23, 28, 89, 98, 101, 105, 106,
   117, 118, 142
trailing (*see* trolling)   113
trevally, giant   17, 122, 126, 127, 141
trolling   29, 35, 56, 68

trolling, flat-line   69
trolling line length   73
trolling lures   56
trolling speeds   56
trolling spoons   69
trout, brook   112
trout (brown)   81, 108, 109, 110, 112
trout, cutthroats   112
trout, lake   112
trout (rainbow)   81, 111, 112, 143
trout (sea)   81, 119
trout, Thames   115
tuna, yellowfin   122, 126
Twin Spin, SR-30 reel   127

unhooking gloves   41
Ure, River   84, 86

Vaughan, Bruce   25, 26, 45
Veltic lures   15, 22, 24, 88
Vibro spoons   22
Vincent, Jim, spoon   23, 28, 85, 87
Voblex lures   24

Wabler lure   76
Wade, Jeremy   86, 140
Wagstaffe, Fred   68
wagtails   22, 23, 25
wahoo   125, 127
Walker, Richard   83, 84
Walker, subsurface   18

walleye   69
Waltham, James   118, 137
water speeds (salmon fishing)   92
weedless spoons   24
Weight, Eric   8, 150
Wessex   104
Weston, Russell   127
wheel   52
Whitehead, Ken (see Deryck Swift)   23, 65, 90, 117
Wilson Flyer (boat)   52
Wilson, John   7
windcheater lure   77
Windermere, Lake   72
Wineglass Bay, Tasmania   143
Winship, Bill   8, 86, 105, 115
winter lure fishing   35
wire cutters   41
wire traces   43, 62, 70, 84, 85, 138
Wissey, River   118
Woodhall, Loch   72
Worldwide Fishing Safaris   152
World Sport Fishing   152
worms   14, 20, 21
Wrasse   133, 135, 136, 142
Wyelead   23
Wye, River   35

yellow-belly lures   95, 118
zander   20, 21, 27, 34, 67